C000131500

PREFACE

The origin of American music has always been something of a mystery. Several proposed explanations unsupported by documented evidence did not prove credible when subjected to close scrutiny. The reason for so much erroneous speculation became apparent when this project began during the final decade of official segregation in the southern States. It was found that meaningful research was extremely difficult because conditions of racism were then unchanged since the Reconstruction years. The solving of the puzzle required a lengthy effort of detection leading through a maze of what at first appeared to be unrelated events.

The history of New Orleans music cannot be separated from the social history of the city. An incorrect assessment of early New Orleans society was a major flaw of previous theories. Research for this work, therefore, was conducted not exclusively from the viewpoint of music but also from the aspect of the social historian.

In former times New Orleans was a social anomaly. The downtown French-speaking section or French Quarter containing an opera house, dance halls and theaters was more sophisticated than elsewhere in America but the manners and customs of the local citizenry were equally strange to Europeans and Americans. In many ways the social life, centered on the dance or *Balle*, was unique. Viewed in this context it seems logical the city would develop a music equally unique.

In organizing the book to follow the convoluted trail of evidence with some sense of orderly arrangement it seemed prudent to divide the material into four sections:

Part I surveys some of the earlier suppositions and dissects the theory of the African origin of jazz, an inconsistent though popularly accepted explanation.

Part II investigates how American music really began and examines why its birthplace was New Orleans. The legal and social environments of the city are also explored in relation to the Creole community.

Part III is intended to illustrate how changing conditions brought a continuing development of New Orleans music. Included in addition is a discussion of the principles of music governing that development.

The final section will be more familiar to those who are acquainted with conventional jazz histories. The aim here, however, is to show how the original music of New Orleans divided into dixieland jazz and swing music. Further, it is intended to indicate that improvised jazz is not a part of the New Orleans style.

Information was gathered from many sources acknowledged in the notes or text. The principle theme was compiled from conversations with hundreds of musicians, active or retired, and from residents of the city far too numerous to list by name. To this multitude of assistants who must remain anonymous much gratitude is tendered. Special acknowledgement should be given to the late Professor Manuel Manetta for generously sharing his memories. A friend for many years the late Bill Russell was helpful in clarifying certain passages from the book *Jazzmen* explained in the text. Appreciation is due to Jane Julian for permission to quote extensively from her translation of *Nos Hommes et Notre Histoire*. A work of this nature must acknowledge Ferdinand "Jelly Roll" Morton (1890–1941) the pre-eminent chronicler of New Orleans music. Views otherwise expressed, of course, are those of the author.

The primary purpose is to relate the events that led to a revolution in music and to retrieve a part of America's cultural heritage. The true history of American music is far more complex than previous fictional versions, a prime example of truth being stranger than fiction. This is the story of a unique American culture and the origin of a distinctively American art form.

adapted for the New Orleans bands, often being played as marches or funeral dirges. The New Orleans style is flexible enough to accommodate all these various modes of music. It was in existence long before church music became stylized, indeed before most churches as we now know them came into being. Church music was played in many places other than New Orleans yet it did not influence music elsewhere, there is no reason to believe it influenced the New Orleans style. Moreover it can be shown that when New Orleans music was in its formative years the city was still a colonial possession where religions other than Catholicism were prohibited.

Finally there have been those perplexed writers who have illogically suggested all these musical influences were involved in the creation of jazz, again with no reasoned explanation why the event should have occurred at one particular time and in one particular location.

CHAPTER 2

THE AFRICAN ORIGIN THEORY

The most pervasive and generally accepted of all the theories to explain the origin of American music is a form of musical Darwinism that assumes it all began in Africa and was brought to America by slaves. The reason for the popularity of this African origin theory is that it seems to satisfy several different and opposing points of view. The southern white racist has been able to refer contemptuously to the music as similar to an instinct residing within creatures from the jungle. Some people devoted to classical music, perhaps more cultured but not necessarily more discerning, have also been able to feel superior. They have proclaimed the exalted status of European music above what they regard as the inferior music from Africa. On the other hand American Black people have pointed with pride to the African culture that supposedly gave birth to the music. And jazz historians have indulged themselves in endless speculation, usually with complete irrationality, on what they have termed the African pre-history of jazz.[2]

As part of the investigation surrounding the African origin theory there have been several expeditions to Africa and various parts of the Americas, notably Haiti, with the aim of disclosing the roots of jazz. Not unexpectedly one or two similarities have been revealed. It has been discovered that drums are used in African music and in American jazz. The fact that drums are used on other continents and in other kinds of music is not usually discussed.

We have been told there is a Call and Response configuration common to both styles of music. Again we are not told the same pattern exists in other music. In European classical music, for example, this pattern is known as the Theme and Answer. Jazzologists apparently do not realize that in New Orleans

8

The break-downs and double-shuffles mentioned in Norman's description is what we would expect of dancers in New Orleans. They are examples of variations that creative people of all races add to the dance to make it more pleasurable. Those who have observed the dancers that accompany the brass bands through the colored districts of New Orleans—the second line— know full well the type of movements to which he refers. Indeed Norman's brief description of the Congo Square dances could just as easily be applied to the New Orleans dancers of today.

Before leaving Norman's report we should comment on his mention of the "green sward." We are not told how many dancers participated in these festivities. The number could not have been large or the grass would not have stayed green for very long. It would suggest not more than a few dozen dancers, perhaps considerably less. Very different from the hundreds or thousands mentioned in the later fanciful reports.

In view of this evidence it seems the Congo Square dancers were really nothing more exotic than a gathering of a few friends, probably servant-slaves of the colonial period, joining together in a neighborhood dance.

Why in a public park?

Surely because it was free, an important factor for those without money. The same kind of thing occurred in Europe where neighborhood people performed their country dances upon the "village greens." Congo Square, it would appear, was simply the village green of New Orleans.

Norman's remarks of 1845 had an interesting sequel. Shortly thereafter the city council passed an ordinance permitting dances in the Square. Previously the slaves were prohibited from such time-wasting activities, but the aim was to show the abolitionist movement that the slaves were really happy and contented. When no happy slaves appeared the *Daily Picayune* indulged in some of the "creative writing" about the slaves which was common at that time. Obviously borrowing from Norman, the newspaper described thousands of Negroes happily doing break-downs on the green sward. Apparently even this was not enough to bring out a single slave though, and we hear no more on the subject.

In 1837 half of the original Congo Park was utilized to build the notorious first parish prison, used under American slave rule as the ultimate tool of oppression for handling the slaves. This was when the park was reduced to a square. Many years later, after the Jim Crow laws of segregation were established, there were reports of dances once again taking place in Congo Square. These reports are by no means authenticated. As we have seen, the 1885 guide book made no mention of such dances being currently performed. But there is a slight possibility some activity may have occurred in the late 1880s. If so it would certainly have been with the use, or misuse, of the police and prison authorities. As the prison was so conveniently located it could have provided the means for presenting a tourist show, of sorts, in the Square. On Saturday night, it is supposed, the police would arrest all the drunks and petty misdemeanor offenders they could find, placing them in the prison overnight. On Sunday morning, closely watched by the police as these reports usually observe, the miserably hungover souls along with several trustee prisoners would be forced to shamble around the square as a condition for their release. It would be a typical southern white bigot joke for some "musical instruments" to be provided by the authorities consisting of "dried bones and casks covered with dried skins" as some reports state.

Those who have experience of police activity in the Black community of New Orleans under the Jim Crow segregation laws know that such a scenario is quite feasible. It should be quickly added that such treatment was relatively humane. Under the earlier rule of the slave system misdemeanor offenders were severely whipped. The newspapers of the time routinely carried reports of such treatment, referring to it with jocularity.

These alleged dancers of the 1880s could not have been slaves. Slavery had long since been abolished and the importation of slaves from the Congo or anywhere else was prohibited by Act of Congress after January 1, 1808. If such "dances" did occur the participants were merely victims of the Jim Crow laws and of the 19th century southern white tourist trade.

Some years later, when the first parish prison was demolished and a new prison erected uptown, a different method was

CHAPTER 5

THE BOLDEN STORY

Buddy Bolden and his small band became famous in New Orleans around the year 1900. All jazz history books have had something to say about this band. It was connected to the African origin fiction again by a single completely unfounded and undocumented sentence in *Jazzmen*:

"The leader of the first great orchestra, Buddy Bolden, was already in his teens before the Congo Dances were discontinued."

This statement is not difficult to refute. Bolden was born in 1877, he would have been thirteen years old in 1890. Twenty-five years after the Civil War abolished slavery and eighty-two years after the United States Congress prohibited the importation of slaves from Africa. "Congo Dances" whatever they may be, never existed in New Orleans during the nineteenth century and Bolden at the age of thirteen would have been almost a century too late to observe even the normal country-style dancing remembered by Mr. B. M. Norman in his guide-book of 1845. Confidently, and it is hoped finally, we may now sever the always tenuous connection between Bolden and Congo Square. Nor was Bolden the leader of "the first great orchestra." He led a small six or seven piece band very similar to other New Orleans bands of that period.

Here perhaps it would not be out of place to dispose of one or two other popular myths about Bolden. He was not a barber although he worked as a plasterer before forming his band on a permanent basis and becoming a full-time musician. He did not edit and publish *The Cricket*, a local periodical circulated in the New Orleans suburb of Algiers. It was an innocuous paper similar to news sheets published in many neighborhoods today.[10] He did not play in an uptown dance hall named Tin Type Hall.

That was an error caused by the New Orleans accent unfamiliar to jazz researchers from the North.[11] There was an uptown hall nick-named Tin *Tack* Hall in which he played at times. These are petty errors which have grown with constant repetition and embellishment to create a false impression of the man.

More serious from our point of view is the false impression of Bolden the musician, and also of his band. Jazz books and books about Bolden invariably refer to him as a Jazzman, the First Man of Jazz, Leader of the First Jazz Band and so on. But at the time of the Bolden band in New Orleans there were no jazz men or jazz bands. During that period and for a number of years after, there were several classifications of bands in the city but the word Jazz did not enter into any of them. For the moment we will not speak of String Bands or Brass Bands, we will concern ourselves only with the Bolden type of dance band. This sort of band divided into two sub-categories. There was the Faker band and the Music band.

The Faker band, as the name implies, was composed of all or almost all, "ear" players. Persons who could not read music and played by ear. The Music band used what was then often called "Musicianers." That is to say persons who could read, understand and play from written music. Skilled journeymen musicians.

By this definition the Bolden Band was unquestionably a Music band, despite all that has been previously written to the contrary.

In New Orleans a Music band, particularly a small one such as Bolden's, did not find it necessary to have the sheet music on a stand in front of them. Because of this they appeared to the casual observer to be a faker band. Once they had learned the piece of music and had it fixed in their minds they were able to play without further reference to the written score. Much the same as a concert soloist at a symphony concert. Unlike that however, in the sense that they were free to create unlimited variations upon the theme. For who would object? Surely not the dancers; they were interested only in good dance music. Music with the correct tempo, a good beat and pleasing to the ear.

Because it is known the Bolden Band was a Music Band

from the first-hand accounts of those who actually played with the band, we can safely disregard much of what has been written. Those who believed it to be a Faker band, while they may possibly have seen or heard it, really knew nothing about the band.

Professor Manuel Manetta played violin several times with the Bolden Band in 1907, replacing his neighbor, Alcide Frank. Although then in his late teens, Manetta was already recognized as a skilled musician and had been playing professionally for five years. He was well aware of the musical competency of the band. Manetta has recalled that Frank Lewis, the clarinetist and acting manager of the band, always had the written music available for any tune the band played.

Mr. Joseph Nicholas, a well-respected musician and music teacher, uncle of the famous clarinetist Albert Nicholas, was several years older than Manetta. He also had no doubts about the ability of the band. He considered "the band could play all kinds of music, every number that was out." After a lifetime of playing, teaching, and listening to music Mr. Nicholas still "liked Bolden better than any in the world."[12]

The testimony of these men and others of similar authenticity leave no doubt this was an excellent Music band composed of competent, highly skilled musicians.

It is not generally understood that in the New Orleans of this period the dance bands, particularly the Music Bands, would always include a violin. The Bolden Band was no exception.[13]

The violinist played the lead part in the band and was expected, and trained, to stomp off the band. As the violin could be relied upon to stay with the straight lead or melody, the clarinet and cornet were released to play variations on the melody. In this way it was possible to have three lead voices in the band which were not playing exactly the same thing but were still fitting within the original melody. Meanwhile the rhythm, key, chord structure and the third-part harmony of the trombone all remained unchanged. In a band of skilled musicians, well rehearsed and familiar with each other's style of playing together, it might even be possible for them to play three different tunes at the same time!

We now see Bill Cornish was not speaking in inexplicable terms with his remark about the Bolden Band, Nor was he referring to anything that may occur in African music. To the contrary he was choosing his words carefully and speaking accurately. He was saying that under the right working conditions:

"When *we* [that is the band] got going good, *they'd* [that is, the three lead instruments] cross three tunes at once." Or play three lead melodies simultaneously.

This is a description of a perfectly normal and acceptable European music form—three part counterpoint. Notice Cornish did not include himself in this three tunes business. His trombone part, along with the rhythm section, was not involved. Nor, in a manner of speaking, was the violin part. That remained with the original melody. So we are left with Frank Lewis on clarinet playing a second tune and Bolden on cornet playing a third tune all within the framework of the first tune. A neat trick—a musical surprise—just the sort of thing that New Orleans musicians have always enjoyed doing, but done in such a way that did not impair the music. No disharmonious sounds were allowed for that would have spoiled the whole effect and rendered the trick useless from the New Orleans musical point of view.

We can begin to get an understanding why the band was so highly regarded by those who really knew it.

Why Frank Lewis was a well respected musician.

Why Bolden became a noted musician in a city of many great musicians.

And why this whole affair had nothing whatever to do with Africa.

It is not intended, nor should it be necessary, to dispute all that has been written about the connection between African music and American jazz. It is hoped enough has now been said to illustrate the fallacies of the African origin theory. With the removal of this last of the basic props perhaps the mountain of academic conjectural rubble will collapse and be allowed to pass quietly into oblivion.

Before leaving Bolden and his band a few more items

28

should be discussed in order to deflate the constantly growing balloon of fiction surrounding the subject.

There are no recorded examples of the three tunes trick. A very simple form of two tunes played consecutively is well known. Presently it is called "quoting." A soloist will insert a few bars of another tune while soloing. In the past it was known as "introducing." This did not mean introducing a new tune, it meant introducing a second tune within the content of the first tune.

The Original Dixieland Jazz Band, The Louisiana Five and other early dixieland bands tried to incorporate several of the musical tricks of the New Orleans bands. These were Faker bands capable only of playing simple repetitive arrangements or "routines." Their records give us a faint idea of what the better bands may have been doing. On a number of their records these bands switched from one tune to a chorus of another tune and back again. This is an elementary example of two tunes within the same rhythm, harmony, key and chord structure but played consecutively. Perhaps a better example is the tune *My Maryland*. Here the trumpet plays one strain of the tune while the band plays a second strain. This musical effect, as with the clarinet solo in the tune *High Society*, is probably a traditional vestige of the New Orleans brass band repertoire. Other examples occur when larger bands play a medley of tunes, sometimes "crossing" two of the tunes in the medley. This, of course, from written scores.

One further example involves the tunes *Dixie* and *Yankee Doodle*. Sometimes a New Orleans colored band, when playing for a southern white audience, would be asked to play *Dixie*. Since this simple ditty is regarded as the unofficial Confederate anthem, the band would say they did not know the tune, thereby losing a tip. At the piano, Professor Manetta found a way to exploit the situation. Combining pragmatism with musical talent he would play *Dixie* with one hand and at the same time play *Yankee Doodle* with the other hand. When this feat won the applause of his listeners he would then stand with his back to the piano and do the same thing, this time reversing his hands on each tune and playing with the backs of his fingers. This might be called compounding the crossing of two tunes.

29

It is well known the Bolden Band could play loudly to attract crowds of people. Not so well known is the fact that the band could also play very quietly, in short, it had a wide range of dynamics. With the full band playing, Bolden's group could play so softly the loudest sound in the dance hall was the swish—swish of the dancer's feet. The contrast was never forgotten by those who experienced it. Manetta remembered Buddy simply turning to the band, gesturing with his hand and saying "Shush—Shush." Some New Orleans dance bands, as opposed to concert or dixieland bands, were still using this effect during the 1950's.

The Bolden band was good-humored and was capable of composing, in part, its own repertoire. Well remembered was the tune called *The Old Cow Died and Old Brock Cried.* A chorus or two of this tune would be sung by the entire band. Intended as a little joke on Brock Mumford, the guitar player, it became a popular tune for the band.

Jazz books have usually described Bolden's Band as an uptown band composed of men who lived in the uptown part of the city. This was only partially true. Downtown men such as Alphonse Picou and Didi Chandler played with the band.[14] And it almost always included men from the suburb of Algiers such as Jimmy Palao, Manuel Manetta, Alcide Frank and Frankie Dusen.

When Manetta was still a schoolboy he got a part-time job to sweep out the Algiers Odd Fellows Hall situated close to the Manetta home. He was given the key to the side door of the hall so he could gain entrance during the day. One night when the Bolden Band was playing there he and a few schoolboy friends sneaked into the hall from the side entrance to observe the band. Manetta was of a musical family so most of the musicians were familiar to him. A man remembered as Peg Leg Ike Isiah was playing the bass fiddle. Brock Mumford was the guitarist and of course Bolden played the cornet. These were all uptown men. But the violinist, Alcide Frank, and the trombonist, Frank Dusen, were from Algiers, close neighbors of the Manetta family. To the great astonishment of Manetta and his friends, however, there appeared to be a young white man playing the clarinet. A situation unheard of in segregated New Orleans. He was later to learn this was Alphonse Picou, a downtown Creole of light color.

It can be seen even in this early band, Bolden would have been only about 21 or 22 years old, there was a downtown musician and two Algiers musicians in the band. Alcide Frank was a regular member of the band having succeeded Jimmy Palao. Dusen played semi-regularly; acting as an agent, he obtained and played on Bolden's Algiers jobs. Picou was substituting for Frank Lewis, the regular clarinet player with the band.

It is often stated the Bolden band played the blues. This is doubtful. Blues were not then popular as dance tunes. It was not until 1912 that the first blues was published, several years after the demise of the band. The blues have always been regarded disdainfully by New Orleans musicians, although not by Fakers, but the band did play slow numbers, Slow Drags, so named because of the slow dragging of one foot in part of the dance movement. These dances may have been mistaken for the blues. The famous *Buddy Bolden Blues* is not a blues but a ragtime strain played slowly. Ragtime music was then at the height of popularity as dance music. It is known the band played ragtime tunes in the manner of a Music band, giving them its own interpretation.[15]

The band did play all the types of dance music then in vogue—Schottiche, Waltz, Quadrilles, Mazurkas and popular tunes. The Bolden arrangement of the then recently published tune *Ida* was a popular number for the band.[16]

Because Bolden was able to assist with a technical problem concerning the bow of his violin, Manetta thought it was possible Bolden had studied the violin. That would not be unusual in New Orleans where a number of violinists (the lead voice in the string bands) doubled on cornet (the lead voice in the brass bands).

Further evidence of the band's ability was their habit of playing a tune "around the belt." The Belt Line was a street car line which pursued a circuitous route. When the Bolden Band played around the belt they played in all the successive keys, returning to the first one. For example, if the band was playing in the key of C, they would switch to D, then to E, eventually returning to the original key. Perhaps to keep the band on its toes, Bolden would sometimes do this quite unexpectedly. As the end of a chorus approached he would suddenly announce "Were going around the belt, look out." On the following chorus the band changed, as a unit, to the next key. After a chorus or two, or perhaps several choruses, Buddy would suddenly yell "Watch it" or some such warning whereupon the band changed to the next key. Playing around the belt was not unique to the Bolden band, other New Orleans bands are known to have employed the devise, but this clearly demonstrates the group must have been a music band.

All who heard Bolden play have spoken of his 'power' his ability to play *forte* to attract a crowd of people. Mr. Joe Nicholas said Bolden would 'shove out' a tune. Not only playing loud but in a driving manner. It is possible the mouthpiece of his cornet had something to do with this power. Playing with the band in 1907 Manetta had the chance to see Bolden's cornet. He observed Bolden using a curious mouthpiece described by Manetta as saddle-shaped. Possibly a custom-made mouthpiece molded to fit Bolden's embouchure. It is generally agreed Bolden must have had an extraordinarily strong embouchure, assisted perhaps by this special mouthpiece. Certainly the loudness of his cornet playing cannot be disputed. When Manetta was listening on the riverfront in Algiers he could hear Bolden playing *inside* Globe Hall in downtown New Orleans, a straight-line distance of considerably more than a mile. The sound traveling across the entire French Quarter and the width of the Mississippi River.

This was a band composed of young men in their late teens and twenties. They were willing to try new ways of approaching their music. They had confidence in their ability to attract crowds and to keep the attention of people. It was not the first jazz band nor an archaic link to mythical Congo Square dances. It was, for that period, a modern New Orleans dance band.

As with all New Orleans music bands, the Bolden Band held regular rehearsal sessions in which new tunes were learned and arrangements for the music were worked out. These rehearsals were held at 1222 Joseph Street the home of Frank Lewis who, as has been noted, seems to have been the manager and guiding light of the band. In a small band such as Bolden's, typically suited for the small neighborhood dance halls, it was seldom necessary to have more than the lead sheets to the music. At times special parts would be arranged and added to the repertoire of the band. This repertoire remained in the possession of Frank Lewis and was always accessible on the bandstand if needed. When Manetta played with the band Lewis always had the music available for him if the band played an unfamiliar tune.

Lewis also seems to have handled the booking arrangements for the uptown jobs. On these engagements Bill Cornish would have played with the band. Frank Duson took the trombone chair for the Algiers and downtown jobs. Duson was a good faker but not a musician, probably one of the very few non-musicians to play with Bolden. Acting as an agent, however, he had a greater value in his ability to find employment for the band.

The famous photograph of the Bolden Band should be discussed briefly. For reasons of his own the photographer posed the guitar and bass in a left-handed position and then reversed the printing of the photo.[17]

The evidence for this conclusion is as follows:

All members of the Bolden band are known to have been skilled musicians who positioned their instruments correctly.

It was traditional for New Orleans bands to have the bass and guitar on the left side of the band.

The trombone and clarinets are held inversely and the clarinet keys are shown reversed.

This evidence is decisive and does not allow for any other interpretation.

Previously, the names of the musicians in the photo were incorrectly placed. From left to right they are: (standing) Frank Lewis, clarinet; Bill Cornish, trombone; Bolden, cornet; Jimmy Johnson, string bass. Seated are Willie Warner, clarinet, and Brock Mumford, guitar.

The strange appearance of two clarinets in such a small band has perplexed jazz writers who have confessed their inability to understand the significance of this arrangement. As we are now aware, the regular personnel of the Bolden Band always included a violinist playing the lead part so it is evident that Warner, seated in the violinist's chair, was substituting for the violin. Warner was a good reading musician who played with the John Robicheaux Orchestra. He would have been quite

The Bolden Band c. 1906. Left to right, seated are Willie Warner, Brock Mumford. Standing are Frank Lewis, Bill Cornish, Buddy Bolden, Jimmy Johnson. Mumford and Johnson are posed artificially in a left handed playing position.

able to play the violin lead parts for the band. When the photo was shown to Manuel Manetta he agreed it would not have been an unreasonable substitution although a little unconventional. Again this is evidence of Bolden's ability to try new ideas.

The absence of drums in the photograph is not unusual for this period. Didi Chandler, also from the Robicheaux Orchestra, is known to have played occasionally with the band but the Bolden Band did not employ drums on a regular basis. As has been mentioned earlier and will be discussed more fully later in the book, drums were a very late addition to New Orleans dance bands. The assumption that the drum was the first or basic instrument of New Orleans bands is a fundamental error of the African origin theory.

In the picture it can also be seen the string bass was played with the bow, the usual method for this period of time. There was no brass bass, tuba or bass horn, used in this band and picking or slapping the string bass, that is, playing *pizzicato*, was not the usual method of playing the bass viol as most of the various dance tempos were then played *legato*.

The Bolden photo was first dated as having been taken before 1895 but it is clear from the ages of the musicians this is not so. Bolden and Warner, for example, were born in 1877, they would have been only seventeen years old in 1894. Jimmy Johnson was born in 1884, he would have been still a child ten years of age. A more accurate date for the picture is 1906 after Alcide Frank, Bolden's regular violinist, had departed the band to form his own Golden Rule Orchestra but before Manuel Manetta, then aged seventeen, had joined the band.

The basic personnel of the Bolden Band seems to have remained remarkably constant throughout the duration of the band. Apart from temporary substitutions the only major changes were the three violinists—Palao, Frank and Manetta— several bass players, and the trombonist Duson who seems to have permanently replaced Cornish in 1907.

Manetta said he was playing with the band on what he believed was the last job played by Bolden. Working at the uptown Love and Charity dance hall in 1907, Buddy suddenly began to play wildly, seeming unable to stop. The other members of the band took him by the hand, gently helping him off the stand, soothing him by saying "There now Buddy, take it easy." Bolden was escorted home and John Pendleton, a local cornet player, was hired to play the remainder of the dance.

A sudden onset of mental derangement may have struck Bolden on several previous occasions but this seems to have been the final blow since he was not known to have played again. Shortly afterward, Frank Duson formed the Eagle Band using several members of Bolden's group, to fill Bolden's engagements. When Duson first formed his Eagle Band it consisted of Edward Clem, cornet; Duson, trombone; Frank Lewis, clarinet; Manetta, violin; Brock Mumford, guitar; Danny Lewis, bass, and Henry Zeno, drums.

In June 1907, only twenty-nine years old, Bolden was committed to the insane asylum of Louisiana where he was to stay for twenty-four years, passing away in 1931.

Charles Buddy Bolden was remembered by those who really knew him as a tall, handsome, well-behaved young man. Very polite in his manner and not a heavy drinker. Manetta insisted Bolden was "a tidy fellow" who bought his suits at a fashionable clothing store on Canal Street and was always neatly dressed. It was not unusual in those days for the musicians of Bolden's band to remove their shirts revealing their blue undershirts when working in the hot, humid dance halls of New Orleans, but Bolden always remained fully clothed. He was well liked by all who had dealings with him which contributed to the success of the band. Employers and managers of dance halls, then and now, prefer to hire musicians and bands that are not only popular and play well but are also well behaved and have pleasant personalities.

The recollections of men who actually played with the Bolden Band leave us in no doubt about two facts: it was a skilled music band and the regular personnel always included a violin player. We are thus able to discard the testimony of those who were not aware of these facts. Unfortunately, this means we must disregard a large percentage of everything that has been written about the Bolden Band. There is the compensatory factor of showing us that it was not a connecting link in the African origin fiction. Instead, we see this was a band directly part of the musical tradition of New Orleans. A little more famous, a little more modern in some of its ideas than many of its contemporaries. Not greatly different though from the dance bands which immediately preceded and followed it in New Orleans, demonstrated by the fact that musicians who worked in the Bolden Band also worked in other bands.

To sum up, the African origin or musical Darwinism theory to account for the beginning of American jazz contains many serious flaws which cannot be satisfactorily resolved. It is based upon incorrect factual information and faulty reasoning. It is defective and simplistic. We are asked to believe that music requiring human intelligence, talent and artistry nonetheless evolved as if it were a mindless part of nature. That it is connected by a chain of circumstances to the African culture of the slaves. The early jazz writers who advanced the theory were not historians; they did not know the importation of slaves to America was forbidden shortly after the end of the 18th century.

In the same way as other forms of human endeavor music does not evolve it is developed and directed by the human mind. New Orleans musicians feel insulted when their musical talents, which they have worked hard to develop, are relegated to the status of an instinct.

Music is a part of human society it will reflect, as do other forms of art, the social conditions surrounding it. The African origin theory did not take this factor into account. The improper premise upon which the theory was founded—that it all began with the slave dancing in Congo Square during the late 19th century—was then followed by woefully inadequate and misdirected research. These initial errors were further compounded by faulty racial assumptions plus a humorous misprint which unfortunately was taken seriously. Finally, there is a continuing misconception of the intrinsic principles upon which New Orleans music is based.

The first researchers were convinced that what they were seeking had little relationship to European music. They were looking for the roots of jazz. Such a revolutionary sound, it was surmised, could not possibly have the same basic principles as conventional music.

37

This judgment has been held firmly, even fanatically by nearly all subsequent jazzologists. When Jelly Roll Morton contradicted their position by stating flatly "Jazz music is based on strictly music"[18] meaning, of course, European music, it earned him the immediate enmity of many in the jazz fraternity. Which is rather strange since it would seem that Morton as a New Orleans musician, composer, arranger and band leader certainly knew more about the subject than any of the establishment critics. When Morton proceeded to prove his words with several musical demonstrations the outrage in some quarters knew no bounds. Because it was not possible to disprove Morton's point the hostility has taken the form of trying to discredit the man, and this unwarranted animosity still persists decades after his death. Morton's thesis, though, along with his music, continues to serenely survive these attacks by lesser talents.

In the many years that have passed since the African origin theory was first proposed nothing of substance has been uncovered that would tend to prove it correct. The theory remains just an unsophisticated and undocumented theory completely without verifiable evidence.

Unfortunately, the original errors of premise and *a priori* reasoning led subsequent jazz research on an entirely wrong course. The result has been the erection of a jazz establishment or "Jazzoisie," as it has been humorously termed, stubbornly clinging to its incongruous social Darwinist theory and resentful of all efforts to rewrite the history of American music in a more accurate form.

Nevertheless, to find a more satisfactory cause for the origin of jazz it is imperative to reject the earlier simplistic theories and turn our inquiries in another direction. Our quest will begin in an age long before the Bolden Band appeared on the scene.

Notes for Part I

1. As an indication of the confusion of ideas concerning the origin of jazz, volume I of a popular reference book of jazz records was dedicated to LaRocca, without whom it said, "there would most probably have been nothing to put in this volume." And in the introduction to volume II of the same work it is stated that ragtime was "the music on which jazz is founded."—Brian Rust, *Jazz Records* (Published by the author, 1961).

2. One author wrote: "Logically, we must place the beginnings of jazz very shortly after Emancipation...Not only was Africa nearer in point of time, but in 1870 freshly landed slaves were at hand."—Rudi Blesh, *Shining Trumpets* (New York: Knopf, 1946, 1958).
Typical of jazz historians who advocate the African origin of jazz theory, this author was not aware the importation of slaves to the United States was prohibited after January 1, 1808 by an Act of Congress March 2, 1807.
Another book, ostensibly concerned with the "Formative Years" of music in New Orleans, included a chapter entitled "Negro Music"(!). However, according to the copious notes there was no consultation with any musicians or New Orleans non-white source of historical information.—Henry A. Kmen, *Music in New Orleans* (Baton Route: L. S. U. Press, 1966)

3. Frederick Ramsay and Charles Edward Smith, eds. *Jazzmen* (New York: Harcourt, Brace, 1939)

4. *Tourist Guidebook to New Orleans.* (New Orleans: Picayune Press, 1909)

5. Will H. Coleman, *Historical Sketch Book and Guide to New Orleans and Environs.* (New York, Self published, 1885), p. 66.

6. J. Curtis Waldo, *Visitors Guide to New Orleans* (New Orleans, Self published, 1875), p. 29.

7. B. M. Norman, *Norman's New Orleans and Environs* (New Orleans, Self published, 1845), p. 182.

8. See for example: Willie Apel and Ralph T. Daniel, *The Harvard Brief Dictionary of Music,* (New York: Washington Square Press, 1961).

9. *Jazzmen*, p. 13.

10. Copies of this paper have been read by the author.

11. The New Orleans accent has caused spelling errors on numerous occasions. The classic instance is Milneburg, a small town named after its founder Alexander Milne. Situated on the shores of Lake Pontchartrain it was first a port for small lake boats. During the late 19th century it was used as a lakefront holiday resort. In the 1930s it was replaced by the present Pontchartrain Recreation Beach. The New Orleans pronunciation is approximately

Mill-'n-burg. Mis-spelled as Milenberg this has led to the strange pronunciation of Mile-en-burg.

12. Mr. Joseph Nicholas in conversation with the author.

13. Many New Orleans musicians, including the eminent clarinetist Emile Barnes, were of the opinion that before the first World War a band without a violin would not be allowed to play for any of the better class engagements in the city.

14. The Creole nickname Didi, also spelled Dede and Dee Dee, translates as "Kid"

15. Ragtime tunes were often written as Slow Drag Two Steps and some were so named or designated, for example the *Sun Flower Slow Drag* by Scott Joplin and Scott Hayden, Joe Jordan's *Nappy Lee*, Joplin's *Palm Leaf Rag, Heliotrope Bouquet* by Joplin and Louis Chauvin, and the five *Pastime Rags* of Artie Matthews.

16. Misquoted in *Jazzmen* as *Idaho,* a popular tune of the 1930s.

17. The reverse printing of this famous photograph remained undetected for twenty years after it was first published. After becoming familiar with the French or Albert system clarinet, invariably used by early New Orleans clarinetists, the author was able to demonstrate the reversed positioning of the hands on the clarinet and of the clarinet keys.

18. Jelly Roll Morton, *Library of Congress recordings,* 1938.

PART II

THE ORIGIN OF
NEW ORLEANS MUSIC

CHAPTER 6

THE CREOLES

To discover the true origin of the New Orleans style of music from which jazz is derived it is necessary to go not to Africa but back into the history of the city of New Orleans itself. Not the sometimes fictional history of tourist guide books. Not the common and often highly prejudiced history of the slave society. Nor the history of the white supremacy post-reconstruction segregated city. These conventional histories are well known but what we seek is more elusive. It is the story of a submerged minority group which has been almost completely silenced to history. We are referring to the Colored Creoles of New Orleans, also known during the slavery years as the Free People of Color or F. P. C.

The true story of these people and their culture is difficult to discover. It is hidden from history because the newspapers, books and print media in general were controlled by the white racist regime. Authentic views could scarcely be expected from such prejudiced sources during the time of slavery and extreme separation of the races. The Colored Creoles, being denied access to print by the slave society, were as effectively silenced to history as were the slaves. The racists of the South seem to have had the purpose of equating the Free People of Color with the slaves, referring to both groups equally as Negroes or, typically, more often as "Niggers."

As a result of these oppressive conditions the culture of the Creoles remains unknown. Yet it is to this silenced society within a society that we must direct our efforts if we would seek to discover the origin of America's music.

The Creole culture was formulated long before American slavery came to Louisiana and it remained different and opposite in viewpoint to the conventional southern society throughout the American slave period.

The French word Creole is thought to be derived from the Spanish word *Criollo*, which meant a new race of people indigenous to the region but of mixed racial descent. The Spanish applied the word to the offspring of a Spanish father and a native American Indian mother. In Louisiana the French settlers applied their word Creole to the offspring of a French father and a native American Indian *or* an African-descended slave mother, apparently using the logic that they were all part of the new race of people being created in the New World.

Over the course of time and with the influx of various European nationalities the word was also used to denote those people, both white and colored, who were descended from French, Spanish, or German settlers. Eventually and inevitably there was a distinction drawn between the white Creoles of European maternity and the colored Creoles but it is by no means certain the original Creoles of either color made that distinction among themselves. They were half-brothers and sisters nursed and raised together in the French household by the Black concubine mother. Brought up under those circumstances racial distinctions would have been impossible and considered to be odious. Indeed there is evidence the Creoles of the French city had great affection for each other regardless of color.

Those feelings were expressed in the foreword to a book written by a New Orleans Creole which will be examined later in more detail:

"I love the Creole of color. I love him above all when he speaks my language for then he is like a close relative. What does the color of his skin matter? ... As a Frenchman I recognise my frame of mind in him and I feel all my sentiments deeply stirred in union with him ...

I love him, my cousin, because he knows how to love; I love him because he knows how to cry ... I have seen mothers wipe away a furtive tear while they spoke to me of the fate which the laws of segregation decree for their children; I have seen strong men wring their hands and cry also, but from anger, at the idea of their complete powerlessness. Then more than ever I have felt that in fact there exists in them a part of myself ..."[1]

In French colonial New Orleans it was legal and customary

44

for the white father to free the slave mother and his children by her. Often this was done posthumously in his will. Seemingly the thought was that he did not want his children or the concubine mother of them to be the slaves of other masters. These children, along with other slaves freed for various reasons, became part of a distinct class of people officially referred to as the *Gens de Couleur Libres* or Free People of Color. Less formally they were known as the Colored Creoles or *Creoles de Couleur*.

It has been a carefully fostered myth of the South that the conditions of colonial slave rule were much more severe than the later slave rule of the American southern states. It does not take a lengthy study of the laws and practices of southern slavery to reveal the truth is exactly the reverse, particularly in the way the laws affected the Free Colored People. The American slave States were determined to eliminate this class of people and in fact some States enacted laws which did so.

Under colonial rule, on the other hand, there was a paternal type of legal system which enabled these people to have almost the same status as the French colonists. They found a place for themselves in the social structure as skilled workers, the artisans of the town, able to make a living performing work that could not be done by the unskilled and uneducated slaves.

As time passed the Creoles became comparatively wealthy, sending their children to France to obtain an education in the same manner as their relatives, the French colonists.

In New Orleans there was always a demand for music. The Creoles were able to fill this demand by becoming skilled musicians. At first the balls at which they played were attended indiscriminately by both the free colored and the white settlers. Toward the end of the colonial period it is estimated the colored Creoles comprised about twenty percent of the free population and there seems to have been little social distinction made between white and colored. Certainly both groups identified closely with the French cultural tradition of minimal racial prejudice.

Because of the artisan role assigned to the colored Creoles in colonial society they eventually formed a characteristic culture of their own. The white Creoles, in contrast, having no need to become productive merely assimilated into the dominant society and never developed an identifiable culture. The diverse history of the two groups make an interesting study in sociology. The colored became industrious, productive and creative, leaving for posterity a new style of music. The whites, wealthy by virtue of their inheritance, became indolent, leaving nothing of cultural value and disappearing into history almost without trace.

France was widely regarded as the cultural leader of the world at this period and since dancing was considered of great importance in French society so also in New Orleans the dance was given a similar emphasis. The journals of visitors to the city repeatedly tell of the balls which were held almost nightly. Significantly, however, there is seldom any reference to the musicians, without whom there could be no dancing. With a few exceptions there is only occasional mention of "a band of music."

By the end of colonial rule all the artisans of the city were Free People of Color. They enjoyed all the rights that were accorded to white citizens and were legally regarded as equals with them. But when Louisiana became part of the American slave system in 1803, the legal environment of the Free Colored People underwent a dramatic change which ultimately was to affect the social environment in a unique manner.

CHAPTER 7

THE LEGAL ENVIRONMENT

In order to understand the anomalous position of the Free Colored Creoles in the New Orleans slave society it is instructive to briefly review the special laws used to govern them. The French colony had a *Code Noir* or Black Code of laws. These laws were primarily intended to regulate the slaves but there were sections pertaining also to their liberation. If a child was born to parents, one of whom was a free person, then that child was also considered free. Any master over twenty years of age could liberate his slaves if he so wished. Under the *Code Noir* laws it was possible for a slave to buy his freedom but the master determined the price. If the price was thought to be too high however, the slave could appeal to the Supreme Council.

Having obtained freedom, the former slaves were given the same rights and privileges accorded to all other free persons. It was required only that the freed slave should show respect to his former masters and that he should not hide any escaped slaves.

In what was still a frontier town there was always a shortage of women. Many female slaves were purchased for the sole purpose of concubinage. It was the usual practice for these women and the resulting children eventually to be emancipated by their French colonial master "for long and faithful service."

With the coming of Spanish rule to New Orleans in 1762 further provisions were made for slaves to obtain their freedom. If a master should use his slave as a prostitute or place his slave in a brothel she could be granted her freedom. Slaves who took Holy Orders or became Priests were given manumission, and a slave who married a Free Colored Person could be given freedom. Throughout the colonial period slaves served in the Militia; those who performed well were usually liberated with the completion of their duty. In these and other ways it can be seen that in colonial New Orleans there was a conscious effort to free slaves and to increase the number of Free People of Color. Furthermore once those people obtained their freedom the society seemed willing to accept and assimilate them.[2]

Colonial laws specifically granted them the same rights, immunities and privileges which were accorded to free-born people. But in 1795, to clarify their position in society, Baron de Carondelet, the Spanish governor, decreed that all Free People of Color were required to work either in the field or at some trade. And he added those who did not do so would be put to work on public buildings. In this way the Free People of Color were encouraged to be productive members of society and many trades were open to them. They became painters, draymen, carpenters, shoemakers, tailors and barbers. Some were butchers or bakers or were employed as servants in hotels. Also some were musicians which was then considered a trade, not a profession.

Although Spanish rule in New Orleans endured for some forty years the town remained French in character. The French settlers, their descendants and the colored Creoles considered themselves to be French citizens speaking the French language and maintaining close ties to France. The New Orleans population never reconciled themselves to Spanish rule, simply ignoring it as much as possible. The Spanish governors of Louisiana soon came to understand the least government of the New Orleans people was the best. Spanish rule frowned upon the French custom of concubinage but they were unable or unwilling to prevent the practice, as a result the number of the Free Colored population steadily increased.

The colonial system of law in Louisiana, partly French and partly Spanish, was comparatively benign to both the slaves and the Creoles. In the French colonies of the West Indies France abolished slavery in 1793. With the return of French rule to Louisiana in 1801 it is virtually certain that had it not been for the American purchase slavery would soon have been abolished in Louisiana also. This situation was duly noticed in the surrounding southern slave states and was a source of concern. Some historians believe if the Louisiana Purchase had been delayed by as little as ten years Louisiana would have had to enter the Union as free territory. A circumstance which would have been a severe blow to the slavery system of the South.

As it was, by 1803 the Free People of Color were of growing significance in Louisiana. Many had become quite wealthy, some even owning plantations and slaves of their own, although under the patriarchal society slaves were considered almost as members of the family and in these instances some or all of the slaves may actually have been members of the family.

With succeeding generations, as the Creoles assimilated into society, it became more difficult to discern the color line. To decide who was a colored Creole and who was a white. It might be said parenthetically that over the years this color line question has been a continuing source of both humor and anxiety in New Orleans. Anxiety among the white community and humor with the colored residents. It led, until recent years, to the sealing of some official records and the vandalist destruction of others to avoid any embarrassing disclosures of ancestry among the citizenry. The point is under the colonial legal system slavery was gradually being phased out of existence in law and in practice.

But with the Treaty of 1803 which brought Louisiana into the Union the legal system began to undergo an immediate and increasingly radical change. The Treaty gave full citizenship rights to all free people without regard to race or color but it soon became clear the Free People of Color were not to receive those rights. Southern white slaveholders and would-be slaveholders poured across the Louisiana borders from neighboring slave states wanting no part of a paternalistic colonial slave system. They lost no time in proceeding to dismantle it.

Black Code laws passed by the first legislatures of Louisiana after the purchase of the Territory were aimed at conformity with other southern slave States. Free People of Color were deprived of voting rights and were forbidden to hold any elective office. Although this was clearly in contravention of the Treaty with France there was no interference by the United States Federal Government or the Supreme Court. The Free Colored People immediately objected to this treatment but their protestations were ignored.

The basic ideology of the slave States was that people of

African descent were little more than beasts of burden. Slaves were no longer regarded as servants; they became valuable commercial property capable of producing great profit for their owners with comparatively little expense. People of Color who were free had to be regarded as an intolerable contradiction to this ideology. The laws of the slave States, therefore, were designed for the purpose of driving the Free Colored population either out of the State or into slavery. The States of Alabama and Mississippi accomplished this by the simple expedient of passing a law saying, in effect, that all Colored People within the State borders were slaves. Period.

In Louisiana, because of the considerable population of former French colonists, it was thought prudent to move cautiously toward this goal. Until the Civil War put an end to slavery the laws were gradually increased in severity until there could be no doubt that slavery or exile for the Free Colored People was the only end in sight. Under French and Spanish rule there had been a mingling of races and an absence of race consciousness, but social equality of the races at any level was totally unacceptable to the American slave system. Above all else the slaveholders feared an insurrection of the slaves and it was thought the Free Colored People could lead such a rebellion. Because of this the Legislature enacted laws with the intent of restricting the growth of the Free Colored population within the State and directed toward the eventual elimination of those people entirely.

In 1806, only three years after the purchase of Louisiana, the legislature of the Territory passed an Act to the effect that the Free Colored People should be required to provide proof they were not slaves. Since many could not show such proof they were arrested and sold into slavery. A year later another Act prevented the immigration of Free Negroes into the Territory. In 1808 a law was enacted that the Free Colored People were to be identified in legal documents as F.M.C. or F.W.C. that is to say Free Men or Women of Color.

After Louisiana became a State in 1812 a series of laws were passed designed to diminish the number of Free Colored Persons. In 1826 an attempt was made to outlaw the French concubinage system so that a white father could not free his colored children. When this failed several Bills were either attempted or enacted in 1830 to accomplish a similar purpose. One unsuccessful Bill would have provided that no slave could be freed unless he was sent to Africa by his owner. But another Bill which did pass into law made slaveholders post one thousand dollars for each slave that was given freedom in order to insure the former slave would leave the state within thirty days.

Legislation passed in 1830 for the expulsion of all Free Colored Persons who arrived in Louisiana after the year 1807. And all Free Colored People who were in the State before January 1, 1825 were required to register at the Mayor's office. Those who entered Louisiana after that date were to leave the State within sixty days of a conviction for any offense.

It became a crime if a Free Person of Color failed to show proper respect to white people. The penalty being three to five years in prison and a fine of up to one thousand dollars. When the prison term expired the offender was to be banished from the State for life.

In addition, what might be called a silence law was enacted to prohibit publication of anything thought to incite discontent among the Free Colored People. The penalty was life imprisonment or execution at the discretion of the court. The same penalty could be imposed on people who held similar kinds of forbidden conversation.

The Louisiana legislature enacted a law in 1842 which ordered that slaves liberated in the future, with certain exceptions, must leave the State permanently. This was followed in 1846 by a law declaring that no slaves were entitled to freedom because they had been out of the State and in a country or State where slavery was prohibited.

By 1857 the legislature was able to pass a law to the effect that no slave could be emancipated in Louisiana at any time in the future. And in 1859 a law was enacted which allowed Free Colored Persons to select their own master and become slaves for life.[3]

These laws were effective in drastically reducing the Free Colored population in New Orleans. The ten years between 1830 and 1840 saw the number officially counted by the census reduced by half. From about 20,000 to barely 10,000.

It is evident from these laws and others of a similar nature passed during the sixty years of American slavery in Louisiana that the intent was to eliminate the Free Colored population entirely. But it is equally clear from newspapers and other contemporary accounts that the laws were unpopular and not strictly enforced in the part of New Orleans which remained French in character.

The city, divided from the first arrival of the American slavers, became increasingly polarized between the uptown Americans and the downtown French. The uptown district became and to this day is still the business and commercial center. The downtown French Quarter remained largely residential and eventually became the part of New Orleans devoted to entertainment, although the Creoles and their culture have long departed the area.

A further hazard to the Free People of Color in the years of slavery was kidnapping. It was not uncommon for gangs of white ruffians to kidnap Free Colored People and sell them to plantation owners as slaves. This form of criminal behaviour was much safer for the kidnapers than horse stealing or cattle rustling. Animal stealing carried severe penalties which were strictly enforced, but whatever laws there were against human stealing were not enforced if the kidnapped person was colored and without the protection of a white master or owner.

Because of this and other predatory acts by whites it became undesirable and even dangerous for the Free People of Color to leave the comparative safety of the French part of town. Furthermore, as whites increased in number with immigrants from Europe, employment for the French-speaking Creoles became difficult to obtain outside of the French Quarter and the Creole section.

The colored Creoles retreated into the isolation of their own society and proceeded to further develop their own culture independently from the rest of New Orleans, the South, and the United States in general. This culture at first was mainly French in nature but with the passage of time it gradually assumed a quality of its own.

The Creole culture of New Orleans.

A culture almost unknown outside of its surrounding and sustaining Creole/French environment.

Perhaps the most distinguishing feature of this culture was the type of music it developed. It was, in fact, a small oasis of *Beaux Arts* within Mencken's Sahara of the Bozart. Or, to put it another way, a tiny island of culture within a vast southern sea of human degradation. A culture ignored and derided in the South and unknown to the outside world.

CHAPTER 8

THE SOCIAL ENVIRONMENT

If we make the assumption that music is an art form and that art reflects society, then if we seek the origin of New Orleans music we must first understand something about the society and the social conditions which gave birth and sustenance to it. To do this it is necessary to briefly review the social history of New Orleans.

The city has often been called a melting pot, a place where people of different nationalities, races and cultures came together. Certainly this was true during the 18th century.

The group of French-Canadian explorers and *voyageurs* who founded the settlement in 1718 were well used to a hardy life in the wilderness of North America. But after New Orleans became the capital of Louisiana in 1723 there must have been a culture shock of sorts when France exported immigrants by the boat-load to populate the crude encampment situated in what was then a cypress swamp.

These were people from the cities, towns and villages of France unaccustomed to life on the American frontier. It is said France emptied its jails to supply a population for its new colony. As women were in short supply in New Orleans prostitutes were a prime target for shipment, but there were also females who voluntarily immigrated. These were the "casquet girls," so named because each girl was given a container of female belongings to help her make a start in the new world.[4]

Some historians have humorously suggested the casquet girls were phenomenally fertile each one bearing at least a dozen children, the prostitutes unaccountably barren leaving no known descendants. In reality the women were eagerly and equally accepted into the community and became the founders of New Orleans first families, although as could be expected prostitution thrived in the seaport.

But this was merely a beginning for soon the growing town saw the arrival of French and Swiss soldiers from Europe and German settlers from locations along the Mississippi River. Members of various religious orders arrived, no doubt to council the number of native Indians which also resided in the town. Add to this motley aggregation a continuing supply of slaves from Africa and it is clear that early New Orleans became the home of many dissimilar kinds of people.

Probably the major influence of this early society was that of the French-Canadian adventurers who were reputed to have had a boisterous nature and a fondness for liquor and women. But a new and radically different element was added to the rapidly growing settlement when in 1743 New Orleans was given a change in Governors.

The first governor, Bienville, had been a French-Canadian *voyageur*, familiar with the rigors of frontier life, but the new Governor had an entirely different background. The Marquis de Vandreuil was from a French aristocratic family and was a member of the Royal Court at Versailles. He began at once to change the face of the New Orleans social order, patterning it after the custom of the French Court.

This period, known to historians as the Little Versailles, introduced the colony to the amusements of French high society. There were fashionable dances, masquerade balls, State dinners and lavish parties, all done in the approved French aristocratic manner and with the prescribed etiquette.

It is known the Marquis was accompanied by a large entourage. In his retinue there were French military officers and members of the French aristocracy along with their families. It would appear reasonable to assume he also brought musicians with him for without them his much-desired dances and masquerade balls were not possible. These musicians probably augmented their income by teaching music, a common practice still in New Orleans.

But who would be their students?

Presumably not many of the white population; the colonial social order did not intend for them to be workers or entertainers of any sort. Not the slaves either, not even if they were merely servant slaves, they were intended for menial and unskilled tasks. Besides, slaves would not have had the education to understand nor the money to pay for lessons.

The logical students would have been the Free People of Color. These were the people intended by the colonial society to perform the skilled work of the colony. Playing music was always regarded in New Orleans as a skilled trade, not a profession, even by the musicians. It would have been recognized as fitting and proper for members of the Free Colored population to learn music. Moreover the oldest of the first generation of colored Creoles would have been approaching their maturity at this time, some twenty years after New Orleans began to be populated as the capital of Louisiana. These and younger Creoles would be seeking a way to earn a living in the niche of the social order open to them.

Music would be particularly attractive to those with talent as it enabled them to have more than one skill and therefore more than one way of earning a living. They could work at a conventional craft during the day and augment their income by playing music in the evening. New Orleans musicians have been doing the same ever since. Only a comparatively small percentage of the city's musicians could make an adequate living solely from music. So it is that here in the middle of the 18th century, along with the maturing of the first generation of colored Creoles, we also have the beginning of the tradition of New Orleans Creole dance music.

The dance music played during this period would certainly have been identical to the music at Versailles, the Allemandes, Courentes, Gavottes, Gigues, Minuets, Sarabandes and various other styles of dance movements which were popular in France. De Vandreuil was not the type of French aristocrat to depart from the Royal tradition.

The administration of the Marquis endured for ten years during which time the idea of French aristocratic amusement permeated the social life of the community. There were an increasing number of balls, private dances, and State parties needing more musicians. A new generation born and raised in New Orleans now replaced the hardy frontiersmen. Being affluent and having no need to work for a living in the slave society they enthusiastically accepted the Marquis' sophisticated ideas of entertainment.

It is not known what happened to the musicians De Vandreuil brought from France. If they stayed in New Orleans surely they would have taken advantage of the opportunities offered by the class and race structure of the burgeoning town. The Marquis' governorship was noted for its patronage system in the same manner as the Versailles Court. It would be surprising if his personal musicians were not given special dispensation so they no longer needed to play music for a living.

Yet despite this combination of more affairs needing music and apparently less musicians available there are no reports of a lack of musicians. To the contrary, there was never a time when New Orleans suffered any such shortage despite the fact that the city had more affairs demanding the presence of music than any other community of similar size. The reason is due to the increasing number of Free People of Color able, willing and even required to supply that demand.

When the Marquis de Vandreuil was promoted to be the Governor-General of Canada in 1753 he presumably took the remainder of his retinue along with him, leaving the colored Creoles to satisfy the need for music in New Orleans. He left a French-American colonial town intensely devoted to the dance. A fertile social environment for the development of a unique music.

It is interesting to speculate on the fate of the French dance music upon which New Orleans music was originally patterned. With the French revolution and the subsequent Napoleonic era the French aristocracy and their culture were obliterated. We can never know what might have happened to the dance music of the French Court. Certainly it would not have developed along the same lines as New Orleans music since it was set in quite a different social environment. In a Royal ceremonial atmosphere it is entirely possible the music may not have shown any indication towards change. It may have become, or stayed rigidly formularized as have so many other types of music.

The musicians of Versailles would have had neither the incentive nor the artistic freedom to experiment which existed in New Orleans. They were playing for the King and his Court, whereas the New Orleans musicians were playing for their relatives and their peers. The artistic environment of the New Orleans musicians would have been tolerant and supportive, they were sure of receiving every encouragement for their efforts. In the Royal Court, on the other hand, probably there was a feeling of indifference, the band being regarded as merely the hired help with no social relationship to the gathering of aristocrats.

Under these vastly different circumstances there is little doubt that whatever might have become of the music of Versailles it would not have developed in the same way as the music of New Orleans.

More than a century later when an astonished world first heard the music of the Crescent City some critics suggested that it came from the brothels of New Orleans. As the licentious practices of the Versailles Court are well known perhaps it can be said those critics were not as wide of the mark as was once thought.

But they had the wrong location.

The next Governor of Louisiana, M. De Kerlerec, had been an officer in the French navy. He seems to have occupied himself mainly with military matters, leaving the Creoles undisturbed in their social affairs. But in 1763 France ceded Louisiana to Spain, causing consternation throughout the colony. When the first Spanish governor arrived in New Orleans the colonists promptly put him on a boat and shipped him back to Spain, declaring their independence. The first such declaration of independence in the New World.

The significance of this act from our point of view is that it shows us the type of people we are dealing with. These second and third generations of Creoles were not bound by tradition. They were not afraid to try something new. This attitude would have been reflected in their social life and consequently in their music. We can be sure it was already undergoing noticeable changes.

After a short period of Creole independence Spain sent an overwhelming military force to New Orleans leaving the Creoles no choice but to accept Spanish rule. It is not known just when the first marching bands appeared in New Orleans. Formerly it was assumed the custom began in the mid-19th century at about the same time as in other towns and cities across America. But as early as 1769 this Spanish force of thousands of soldiers may have brought some type of military band with them to parade around the town and intimidate the populace.

This gesture of defiant independence by the Creoles, the first on the American continent, had a much wider meaning among the colonial powers of Europe. It was greatly feared the idea might spread to other American colonies. Certainly Spain thought it important enough to send twenty four ships, three thousand soldiers and many artillery pieces to subdue the colony, a major undertaking for those days. Spanish authorities realized they were handling a hot potato in trying to govern these fiercely independent Louisiana Creoles yet it was vital to quickly placate the colony. They decided to adopt a conciliatory attitude. To let the Creoles enjoy themselves in their own way and so forget all thoughts of rebellion. This would have been an ideal environment to allow for artistic freedom in the development of Creole music.

When the military occupation ended the Spanish appointed the young and handsome Don Louis Unzaga as Governor. He lost no time in marrying a Creole beauty, thereby soothing the ruffled feathers of everyone concerned. His officers and men, following his example, also promptly married Creoles, probably of varying colors. It would seem the Spanish were under orders to integrate themselves into the community as quickly as possible to reduce the chance of any further uprisings. Spain had no desire to mount another large and expensive military operation against these pesky Creoles. It was imperative to bring calm to the city and to allay the fears of the citizenry. A new chapter now began in New Orleans cultural history. Spanish domination was bound to bring profound changes in the social environment and those changes inevitably would be reflected in the music.

The Creole insurrection was not totally a lost cause. Through a succession of Governors, Spain was careful to provide the town with competent and co-operative administrations. New Orleans settled down to an uneasy, though peaceful, truce. For the next thirty years the Creoles were in a curious position. They continued to use French as their language and kept in close contact with France but they no longer had any official standing at Versailles. After the great upheaval of the French revolution in 1789 the resulting Republic of France, busy with its own problems, failed to show much interest in the affairs of Louisiana.

It was during this period that two great fires swept through New Orleans destroying the old wooden French buildings. The Spanish administration rebuilt the town using brick construction and Spanish architecture leaving the "French Quarter" more or less as it stands today, that is, Spanish in appearance.

With control of the city taken out of their hands, the Creoles retreated within their own society. Their devotion to the dance continued unabated and in the 1770s there is mention of it from an unexpected source. In 1772 a group of Spanish Capuchin monks arrived in New Orleans. It seems the Cuban authorities of the Order had heard of some unconventional activities in the town and wanted to know how it had affected, or corrupted, the French Capuchins. In his report to the Havana headquarters the leader of this group was critical of the New Orleans Capuchins but on one point he could be reassuring. He wrote:

". . . as to their going to balls, I do not see any probability of it as the youngest of them is fifty years old; but they frequently attend dinner parties . . ."[5]

It can be seen from this offhand remark that despite changes in governments and ruling countries, rebellions and fires, destruction and construction of the town, the tradition of the dance De Vandreuil began a quarter of a century earlier was continuing apace. The fame of the New Orleans balls, it seems, had spread to Cuba, disturbing the solemn Monks. A situation which was to be repeated several decades later when the puritan-minded American slavers also became disturbed at the Gallic amusements of New Orleans. By this time, it may be safely assumed, the music had diverged considerably from the original pattern to match the momentous events which were taking place in the city.

Throughout this period there are no reports of any Spanish musicians arriving in town. The Spanish Government may have

Uptown New Orleans in 1852. The arched columns of the new (American) City Hall are visible at the left.

they were expected to play concerts probably consisting of popular operatic arias and classical music. Clearly these were highly skilled and versatile French-Creole *musiciens* or "musicianers" to use the later Creole-American term. As previously pointed out, under the colonial class system there can be no doubt they would have been colored Creoles.

On December 20, 1803, three weeks after the departure of the Spanish, Louisiana became part of the United States. This did not mean the Creoles regained control over their own affairs, for now the American slavers saw to it that Louisiana became part of the Southern States' slave system. Politically out-maneuvered and unfamiliar with the language of their new rulers, the Creoles tended to remain secluded within the downtown area. Meanwhile the Americans moved up-river, across Canal Street, and quickly began to build a new part of the city. The uptown American business district.

The old colonial division of labor was supplanted by the southern American system of commercial slavery and the colored Creole merchants and artisans were increasingly displaced by the American and immigrant labor which began to flood into New Orleans. As the town expanded the white Creole population moved further downriver across Esplanade Avenue into what had been the Marigny plantation. The Colored Creoles moved more to the rear of the town across what had been the ramparts of the colonial town and now became Rampart Street. For many years during the 19th century this rear portion of downtown New Orleans was known as the Creole section and was so named on some maps of the city. It can be noted there are some descendants of the colored Creoles still living in this part of the city, still proud to call themselves Creoles.

The American slave system put the Creoles of color into a situation of legal, social and even physical isolation. In this enforced virtual exile the Creoles had little choice but to retreat within their own cultural environment. Being excluded from the prevailing social order they began to form their own social clubs and to build their own meeting halls, which of course, were also used as dance halls. Among the earliest of the Creole societies of which we have knowledge were *Les Artisans* a society founded in 1834, *L'Economie et Mutuelle Aide Societe* organized in 1836,

Les Francs Amis (Free Friends) and the Friends of Hope Society. These Mutual Aid and Protection societies arose partly in response to the repressive laws then being enacted against the Free People of Color. Before the age of trades unions and insurance companies these local societies were a means of affording some protection to the oppressed minority. They also offered a way for the colored Creoles to preserve and develop their culture.

During the next several decades a large number of local societies were formed both for the Free Colored and for the white people particularly the Masons and the immigrants. Later we shall have more to say about these neighborhood dance halls built in the 19th century. For now we should note that it is in these halls that the music style of the European colony, already greatly changed from its original form, became that of America. More precisely it developed into the distinctive style recognized today as New Orleans music. A music style unlike any other previously known anywhere on earth.

CHAPTER 9

A WINDOW OF HISTORY

The laws passed during the sixty years of slave rule in Louisiana were very effective in silencing the colored Creole society to history. Because they were not allowed access to print and because their language was French, little is known of the Creoles in that time of severe oppression. To the researcher it sometimes seems as if their historical record is a frustrating blank wall. Yet in that wall there does exist a small window of Creole history in print although it is almost unknown and has been ignored for the most part. In this chapter we intend to peer through that window in an endeavor to bring some light of understanding to a hidden and forgotten minority culture.

After the Louisiana Purchase, when slavery became commercialized and the division between the races drastically widened, racial intolerance increased to such a degree the Creoles of Color could no longer easily interact with their white Creole relatives. Although the Colored Creoles still supplied the music for the various social events of the whites, they were excluded from actual participation. For example during the winter of 1825–1826 the Duke of Saxe-Weimar, Eisenach, visited New Orleans and recorded the following impressions:

"No day passed over this winter which did not produce something pleasant and interesting . . . dinners, evening parties, masquerades and other amusements followed close on each other.

There were masked balls every night of the Carnival at the French theater which had a handsome saloon well ornamented with mirrors with three rows of seats arranged *en ampitheatre*. Tuesdays and Fridays were the nights for the subscription balls where none but good society were admitted. The ladies are very pretty, with a genteel French air, their dress extremely elegant after the latest Paris fashion; they dance excellently. Two cotillions and a waltz were danced in quick succession; the musicians were colored and pretty good . . ."[7]

The surprise here is not so much that the Duke thought the New Orleans musicians were "pretty good" but that he bothered to take any notice of them at all. In those days musicians were thought to be in the same category as servants. For them to have made an impression on the Duke which he felt was worthy of written comment can be regarded as high praise. The point is, this report clearly indicates the musicians were the only colored persons present at these balls.

Not only were the colored Creoles denied access to the social events of the white people other than supplying the music, they were also denied public education although they continued to be taxed for it. In response they were forced to establish their own schools and to educate their children privately. With good reason they regarded France, not the United States, as the land of freedom so the more wealthy among them sent their children to France to continue their education. Some of these persons stayed in France and pursued illustrious careers, becoming quite well known. Others managed to achieve some distinction in New Orleans despite the difficulties of race prejudice.

Much of what we know of these people during this period comes from a remarkable book, written in the French language, authored by a Colored Creole named Rodolphe L. Desdunes. Entitled *Nos Hommes et Notre Histoire* (Our Men and Our Story) the book was published in Montreal in 1911. Within its covers the author tells something of the history of the Creoles of Color and mentions the names of more than a hundred men and women who became prominent in New Orleans Creole society. In addition, he included brief sketches of the lives of several of the more famous and accomplished among them. This book of Desdunes will serve as our window to observe the Creole people during the epoch of slavery in New Orleans.[8]

Beginning with the war of 1814–1815, our Creole historian tells of the colored Creoles who fought against the British side by side with the Americans in the Battle of New Orleans. We are told of a veteran of that action, Hippolyte Castra, and his recounting, here translated, of how the colored Creoles were regarded by the society they had fought to preserve:

The Campaign of 1814–1815

I remember that one day in my childhood
A fine morning, my mother sighing
Told me, "Child, emblem of innocence,
You don't know the fate which awaits you.
Under this fine sky you believe you see your Fatherland.
Turn away from your error my darling boy
And above all believe your dear mother
Here you are only an object of scorn."

Ten years later, over our vast frontiers
The cannon of the English are heard
And then these words: "Let us run to conquer, my brothers,
We are all born of Louisiana blood"
At these sweet words, embracing my mother
I followed you, repeating your cries
No longer thinking, in my warlike course
That I was only an object of scorn.

Arriving on the field of battle
I fought like a brave warrior
Neither the cannon balls nor the grapeshot
Never, never, were able to frighten me
I fought with this valor
In the sole hope of serving you my country
Not thinking that for my reward
I would be only an object of scorn.

After having carried off the victory
In this terrible and glorious combat
You have, when drinking, made a toast
Calling me a valorous soldier.
I, without regret, with a sincere heart
Alas! I drank, believing you my friends

70

No longer thinking that for my reward
I would be only an object of scorn.

But today I sigh with sadness
Because I perceive a change in you
I don't see the gracious smile any more
which was shown so often at other times
With brightness on your honeyed mouths,
Are you becoming my enemy?
Ah! I see it in your angry looks
I am no more than an object of scorn.

This poem of Hippolyte Castra is the earliest work of French-Creole literature yet surfaced to research. Earlier works are probably indistinguishable from the general Louisiana-French literature. It is followed by a lengthy period of silence until 1845 when a small book of poems was published by private subscription. The title of the book, *Les Cenelles*, refers to the fruit of the Hawthorn. With his customary delicate phraseology Desdunes says of this poetry book: "Its small size tells of the modesty of our writers and the hawthorn, a shrub-like thorny tree with white and colored flowers expresses, I believe, the difficulty of the enterprise for those who had to work in surroundings unfavorable to their poetic tendencies."

Another interpretation might be that the allusion to the bitter fruit of a thorny plant is an allegorical reference to the sad results of American slavery upon the Creole people.

Seventeen colored Creoles have poems in *Les Cenelles*. Desdunes sometimes calls them Creoles of Color, but often refers to them simply as Creoles or Creoles of Louisiana. It can be assumed the white Creoles had integrated into the American community no longer distinct as Creoles, but simply as (white) Americans.

Of this book of poems, Desdunes says further:

"It must not be forgotten that *Les Cenelles* was written and published during the epoch of slavery and that because of the restrictive laws and social prejudice those who collaborated on it did not enjoy the same advantages as other men.

Considered from a philosophical point of view the work of

Les Cenelles presents a triumph of the human spirit over the forces of obscurity. For, in Louisiana there is no lack of people who oppose the education and the development of intelligence among the masses of color."

In his book our Creole historian gives us short accounts of the lives of some of those poets and other Creoles. What follows here is translated, condensed and occasionally quoted from those accounts. It is hoped in this way to gain some knowledge and understanding of the Louisiana Creoles and their culture at the time when they were subjected to the oppressive laws of the slave system.

We begin with Professor Armand Lanusse. This man lived from 1812 to 1867; unlike many literate Creoles he did not go to France for a higher education, he was educated in New Orleans. Lanusse was a poet, a student of the French language, and from 1852 to 1866 a teacher and principle of the Mme. Couvent school. This school, founded in 1832 by a grant of property in the will of Mme. Couvent, a Black woman, was originally intended for the education of the orphans of the Free People of Color. It was then named The Catholic Institution of the Indigent Orphans. Later the school accepted children from all Creole families with a small charge for those who could afford to pay. It is noteworthy that the name of this institution has been preserved for there is still a Couvent school downtown, within the New Orleans school system. When the school opened about 1848 after a long legal struggle, the teachers, in addition to Lanusse were Joani Questry, Constant Reynes and Joseph Vigneaux. The founding of this school for colored children in New Orleans during the time of slavery was considered a very large success for the colored Creoles.

It would appear Lanusse played a large part in the stratagem which resulted in the publication of *Les Cenelles*, possibly he allowed the publisher to believe he was white. Such situations were fairly common in New Orleans but typically the Creoles of this period did not usually try to pass for being a white person as they were proud of their ancestry and their culture. Lanusse is believed to have had a hand in the publication of *L'Album Litteraire, Journal des Juenes Gens, Amateurs de la*

Marie C. Couvent public school in downtown New Orleans.

Litterature, a French-language periodical of poems and articles designed to alert the Creoles to the dangers of increasing discrimination. After the Civil War, with the Union occupation of New Orleans, Lanusse turned to politics, writing for the colored newspapers of the city.

Desdunes tells us:

"The contemporaries of M. Lanusse loved literature, painting, music, theater, games, hunting, all the imaginable genres of pleasure. They applied themselves incessantly to invent new recreations. It is thus that the banquets, the baptisms, the holiday of the first communion were so much to the taste of our former population. Marriages were also the occasion of joyous behaviour. Gambling was inevitable in social gatherings. No one took an interest in the cause of humanity because they did not believe the abolition of slavery was possible in the near future. A great number of persons of color even owned slaves. All this means that the gatherings, although frequent and of different nature, were not of any importance for society with regard to justice and liberty ... It is thus very natural that M. Lanusse in his literature reflects the view, the customs, the sentiments and the inclinations of his contemporaries. This patriot, seeing only poets around him, was not able to do otherwise but to think with them. Naturally he dreamed of seeing poets in the future, not politicians.

He could not attack slavery, or at least deplore its existence, because his friends made no mention of it in *Les Cenelles*. In other words he could not in any fashion make himself an agitator because he would have been the only one to agitate."

After the Civil War Lanusse did become an "agitator" as did many Creoles, striving for civil rights until his untimely death in 1867. In this passage Desdunes explains why the Creoles were disposed to the intense development of their culture, the "genres of pleasure" including music, knowing that as a small minority group they were not able to achieve the abolition of slavery by themselves.

M. Lucian "Lolo" Mansion was a wealthy cigar manufacturer and an excellent poet but his work does not appear in *Les Cenelles*, perhaps because his poems were too critical of slavery.

One of his lighter composition entitled "La Folle" did appear in the *Athene Louisianais*, a white Creole publication. During the 1850s, when the Creoles were being rigorously persecuted, he spent part of his fortune in arranging for many Creoles to escape to Haiti and Mexico.

The Creole best known to researchers is Paul Trevigne because he was an editor of, and a writer with a number of newspapers during and after the Reconstruction period. Born in 1825 the son of a veteran of the 1814–1815 Battle of New Orleans, he lived to the age of eighty-three. Fluent in several languages, for forty years he was a teacher in downtown New Orleans. He was the editor of the Creole newspapers *L'Union* and its successor *The Tribune*, to which he contributed many stirring articles incurring the wrath of southern whites to the point of his being threatened with jail from the floor of the Louisiana legislature. He also wrote for *The Louisianian* and later became the contributing editor of *The Crusader* a bi-lingual post-Reconstruction newspaper.

Desdunes says:

"Mr. Trevigne had a correct style and a flowing composition; his writings were satirical. He chastised while laughing. Perhaps this playful manner which he had of expounding his ideas and his commentaries served to spare him from disagreeable reprisals especially during the time when the whites were little accustomed to accept the opinions of the men of color. Nothing lit the fire of indignation in the democrat more than the sight of this man of color taking his place in the intellectual domain. All that this man could say, do or write to defend his rights, accept his progress or prove his merit was qualified by the other as impertinence, aggression or audacity. Thus, the hate against a man like Mr. Trevigne was intense and always broke out at the lightest friction.

Mr. Trevigne died at eighty-three and perhaps because of his long life he was permitted to traverse the great crises of our country. He was born and reared during slavery. Instructed and gifted with a high intelligence, he was able to follow and judge the events which unrolled before him. He saw the men, women and children of his race sold; he saw them whipped, and often he saw them suffer and die in chains. Later he saw the dawn of liberty, and this transition gave birth in him the desire to make his fellows benefit from the experience of his life. He did that, and the Creole people owe him a place among their immortals.

The men of his epoch honored him with their confidence; he justified this confidence as far as he was able . . . There are perhaps in the people more remarkable men than Mr. Paul Trevigne, but his unique position recommends him a distinction which could not be given to any other of his compatriots . . ."

Eugene Warbourg was born in New Orleans about 1825, "a free man of color, child of foreign parents," and died in Rome, Italy, in 1861. He became an apprentice sculptor to a French artist named Gabriel who had an establishment on Bourbon street. Soon Warbourg became an expert sculptor and opened his own place of business on St. Peter street. His brother Daniel also became a sculptor and engraver with an adjoining business address.

Warbourg did busts of Generals, Magistrates and other notable subjects and did works for the St. Louis Cathedral. Many of the remarkable monuments and statues in the New Orleans cemeteries were done by this man. In 1852 he traveled to Paris where he stayed for six years, then he went to Belgium, London, Florence and finally Rome. Of the many Louisiana Creoles that achieved distinction in Europe, Warbourg was one of the most famous.

The Creoles were not without their painters. Alexandre Pickhill is compared with Titian, Desdunes writes that Pickhill executed magnificent paintings and was perhaps the best painter of his epoch. Because of his disillusionment and despair with the slave society he became morose and destroyed all of his work, leaving nothing to posterity; not the only Creole artist to have eventually committed this sort of artistic suicide while trying to survive within the cultural desert of slavery. Pickhill died in New Orleans about 1845.

For more than forty years before the Civil War Joseph Abeilard was an architect of some renown in Louisiana. Desdunes remarks: "He could draw up a plan like an architect, appreciate the qualities of materials like a workman, draft and observe the stipulations of a contract like a contractor and execute with his hands the diverse parts of a work like the best practicing tradesman."

Often, in the typical way of the South, he had to subordinate himself to an inferior white architect who then collected the fee for the project, leaving the work to the Creole. Joseph Abeilard lived all his life in New Orleans. His brother Jules was also an artisan of the first rank who went to Panama where he died, Desdunes says: "Leaving a heritage of a beautiful and enviable reputation."

Professor R. J. Edmunds was a mathematician educated in France. During the Reconstruction period the Bureau of Public Schools in New Orleans invited him to occupy the chair of Mathematics Professor. When he accepted the post he was attacked in the white-owned newspapers on the usual grounds of race inferiority. Desdunes recounts how the Professor handled the situation: "To put an end to these worries of which he was the subject, the Master issued a challenge to all his detractors, inviting them to come and encounter him at the blackboard. After that he was left alone . . ."

Unhappily, following an illness and while still a young man, Professor Edmunds lost his reason and remained mentally incapacitated until his death. *The Louisianian*, a newspaper we will consult later in this book, carried a laudatory article about Professor Edmunds on September 18, 1875.

Norbert Rillieux was the most famous of the Creoles in the 19th century. Desdunes wrote: "We have had heroes, writers, musicians, painters, sculptors and architects, but Rillieux was a scientific genius."

In Paris Rillieux had been the highly respected head of the *Ecole Centrale*. In Louisiana he is best remembered for his invention of the vacuum-pan centrifugal apparatus, a process that revolutionized the production of sugar and was instrumental in creating vast fortunes for the owners of slave plantations. Rillieux is believed to have submitted the first plans for the modernization of the drainage system of New Orleans, only to have them rejected on grounds of race prejudice.

After his death he was eulogized in the New Orleans newspapers but as Desdunes notes, those papers "were careful not to make the least allusion to his origin. Every intelligent man understands the reason for this odious reticence: it is because it was a matter of removing from the Creoles the glory which they could draw from this illustrious personality."

The Creoles also had their doctors. Doctor Oscar Guimbillotte was born in New Orleans in 1831, the son of a Frenchman and a woman of color. In appearance he was white, with chestnut hair and blue eyes but he married a colored woman and lived as a Creole of color. Besides being a well-respected doctor he was a botanist and a well-read man of letters, having been educated in Paris. For more than twenty-five years he attended the sick of both races in the city. He died aged fifty-five on January 21, 1886.

Alexander Chaumette was another Creole doctor born in New Orleans and educated in Paris. Although he possessed a French diploma and had served in the hospitals of Paris he was subjected to a rigorous and humiliating examination of his credentials by the white doctors of New Orleans before he was finally admitted to the practice. Eventually the medical fraternity recognized his ability and he also attended the sick of both races.

The brothers Adolph and Armand Duhart were associated with the Couvent school. Adolph was educated in France and later became a Principle of the school, succeeding M. Questry. He was considered to be a gifted poet and authored a play entitled *Lellia* which was staged at the Orleans Theater about the year 1867. Armand was a skilled printer and known as a man of letters. He was a director of the Couvent institution and a member of the *Union Louisianaise* founded in 1884 to aid the Couvent school.

A versatile Creole who lived all his life in the city was Basile Croquere. Besides being a poet Croquere was a teacher of mathematics and an artisan carpenter. He and his friend Noel

J. Bacchus were the two cleverest builders of staircases. It is known that many of the plantation mansions were designed and their construction supervised by Creoles; we may assume these two men built some of the handsome staircases which graced the interior of those homes. But it was as a "Master of Arms" that Croquere achieved his greatest fame.

Before the Civil War New Orleans had a considerable number of experts at fencing and dueling. It was generally conceded that Croquere was the best of all. His fame as a swordsman drew mention in a history of Louisiana written by a white person wherein he was termed a mulatto. Desdunes does not fail to point out the insult of the word and states Croquere, in fact, was three-quarters white. In the extremely color-conscious South such distinctions, understandably, had importance to the Creoles. As to Croquere's swordsmanship, Desdunes writes: "He could *touché* his adversary while composing a ballad . . . he often said that his breast was a *point sacre*. It would seem so for it is affirmed that the foil of an adversary never touched it. Moreover Croquere had the good fortune, like his most esteemed compatriots, to understand that work, even manual labor, is a treasure . . ."

This statement is worth noting for it is not possible to understand the Creoles as a class of people unless it is realized they thought of themselves as artisans, or highly skilled independent craftsmen. This is the attitude they brought to their music and with that practical approach they were able to bring innovation, always with the aim of enriching the innate beauty of the music. Creole musicians felt under no obligation other than to produce good music pleasing to the public. The driving force was the competition among themselves to play the best music and so obtain the best and highest-paying engagements.

Desdunes writes of other Creoles who became famous swordsmen or Masters of Arms. The most well known were Robert Severin, M. St. Pierre, Joseph Joly and Joseph Auld. He adds: ". . . These fine blades were the companions of the great master and had more than once crossed iron with him . . . personally M. Croquere was charming. His correct and lucid conversation made him in demand by society . . . Basile Croquere contributed visibly to the prestige of the Creole people."

Among other Creoles named in Desdunes' book are the philanthropists. Georges Alces, the owner of a large cigar-manufacturing business employing more than two hundred people. Alcide Labat, remembered for his support of *The Crusader* a newspaper with which the Creoles were involved. Julien Dejour, a slater: "This young man created an enviable position by his work but in proportion as he earned money, he gave it to the unfortunate ones whom he knew to be needy. The white, the black, the yellow, all were the same to his eyes, and all received marks of compassion from him and considerable aid." Aristide Mary, one of the most respected Creoles of the post-Civil War period, was not a wealthy man but: "He never refused to distribute his money to the needy, within the measure of his means."

Probably the wealthiest of all the colored Creoles was Thomy Lafon, reputed to be worth almost half a million dollars at his death, an enormous sum for those days. He was also the greatest of the Creole philanthropists. Born in New Orleans of a French father and a Haitian mother, he is said to have spent his childhood in poverty but later became a businessman and a financier. Among the many charities for which he was remembered were The Asylum for the Aged, a Boy's Home, The Convent of the Holy Family, and The Juenes Amis (Young Frienda) Society. ". . . his philanthropy extended to all classes of society. The State, the church and charity, all received benefits without regard to color or race, sex or age. Although Lafon was Catholic, he was more concerned with the fate of an unfortunate man than with religion. He was as modest as he was generous. He always desired silence about his good works. He was a true philanthropist . . ."

Desdunes' history of the Creoles is entitled "Our Men and Our Story" but as a true Creole *galant* he does not forget to speak of the Creole women. Before modern drainage and sanitation methods came to New Orleans there were frequent outbreaks of yellow fever, cholera and other deadly diseases. The Creole women became famous for their competence in dealing with those who suffered. Their ability to nurse the sick back to health earned them the Creole name of *femmes traiteuses*, that is, women who could cheat death of its victims. As the diseases did not usually afflict those who were acclimated to New Orleans it was ironic the Creole nurses were often called to attend the newly arrived American slavers who had so little respect for the colored people.

During the years of repression there was nothing that annoyed the Creole people more than the attacks and innuendoes made by white writers upon the devoutly religious Catholic Creole women. Repeated tales of the loose morals of Creole females were infuriating to the Creole population; stories of Creole women seeking white males at "Quadroon balls" and of Creole girls kept by wealthy young white men in "little houses on the ramparts." These slurs on the morals of Creole women disgusted the Creoles but as a severly oppressed and silenced minority there was little they could say or do. This is by no means intended to suggest that prostitution did not exist in the city. Far from it. New Orleans, as all major seaports, has always had a large amount of prostitution. Under the slave system, however, colored prostitutes were urban slaves. They were the property of white pimps and were driven into prostitution for the benefit of their masters. Competition of any kind was not tolerated by these wealthy and politically protected pimps.

The colonial laws of Louisiana could grant freedom to a slave forced into prostitution but the American slave system ignored such conduct. When interested parties were paid off in accordance with the accepted corrupt practices of slavery no official notice was taken of the activity. Occasional small time free-lance operators, of course, were quickly arrested and prosecuted.

Neither the southern press nor the literature of the period made any disclosure of organized slave prostitution. The distorted puritan ethics of the slave South could not allow public admittance that slave prostitution and slave-master pimps even existed. If this seems unlikely it should be remembered the slave system of society was not a democracy; it was more in the nature of a large scale conspiracy. The ballot was restricted to wealthy white landowners and merchants. In addition, the hypocritical Victorian morals of the 19th century were not inclined to accept organized prostitution as a suitable subject for publication. With those conditions the virtuous reputation of the deeply religious Creole women was turned against them. Some white males preferred to falsely boast of their conquest of Free Colored Creoles, famous for their beauty, than to admit to relations with slave prostitutes.

Southern writers of romance books never tired of spinning yarns of forlorn Creole women yearning for their white lovers. Of Creole girls destined to be broken hearted because the mores of society would not allow them to marry their white paramours.

The truth was more prosaic. Among the Creole people throughout the American slave period there were feelings of aversion and revulsion for the boorish white oppressors. The attitude and actions of the slave society left no doubt in the minds of anyone that the whites were determined to eradicate the Free Creoles and their culture. The majority attitude was contempt not love, for colored people and rape was the more common occurrence, although when rape was committed by a white male against a colored female it was not considered to be a legal offense.

Those history books of New Orleans written by southern white supporters of slavery invariably described the "Quadroon balls" in romantic terms. A situation which in itself should make us suspicious for there was nothing romantic about the race relations of American slavery. In reality the balls were a devise used by the white pimp slave masters as a way of promoting their particular type of slavery. The object of the balls was to bring together the colored slave prostitutes and the white male customers. It is certain Free Creole women would not have wished to attend such dances. It is equally certain the white pimp slavers would not have allowed any women other than their own slave prostitutes to take part in the affairs.

The "houses on the ramparts" were houses of prostitution under control of the pimps, located in what was then the unofficial red-light district. Later, when the Jim Crow laws replaced those of slavery, the area became the legally established red-light district of New Orleans, about which we shall presently have more to say.

The prostitution aspect of slavery, in the same manner as many other sordid activities of slave society, had very little to do with the Creoles. In their isolated position they took pride in caring for their own people, indeed if they wished to save their culture and themselves they had no other choice.

In his chapter concerned with the Creole women Desdunes tells of Henriette Delile. This pious Creole woman was instrumental in establishing several churches in New Orleans but she was remembered most for founding and becoming the first Mother Superior of The Society of the Holy Family. This religious Order, still in existance, served as a refuge for widows and destitute Creole females "who wished to retire from the world and live in tranquillity and meditation." It was founded, as Desdunes writes, with "an entirely charitable purpose whose aim was to nourish, to lodge and to take care of the needy of the Creole population." Precisely so, and because the Creoles were able to take care of their own people they achieved a small measure of independence from the surrounding human depravity.

Among other Creole women mentioned by Desdunes were Mme. Louisa R. Lamotte and Mlle. Virginia Girodeau. Mme. Lamotte spent many years in France, eventually becoming the head of the *College de Juene Filles* of Abbeville. She was decorated by the French government with the prestigious *Palmes Academiques*. On her return to New Orleans she was associated with the newspaper *L'Abeille* which publicly expressed profound regrets upon her death in 1907.

Mlle. Virginia Girodeau was an actress and opera star, considered to be a great tragedienne and a leading performer of the New Orleans stage. She is believed to have studied in France under the direction of M. Perennes, a famous French professor of the 19th century. In New Orleans she was remembered for her performances at the *Theatre de la Renaissance*. This was a combination theater and ballroom built and operated by the Creoles, situated at the corner of Champs Elysee and Grand Hommes Streets in downtown New Orleans. The theater opened in 1840 featuring vaudevilles, comedies, opera-comiques, dramas and tragedies in addition to dances and concerts.

Desdunes writes of Mlle. Girodeau:

". . . because of this she had the right to see her name left to posterity and surrounded with all the respect due to her recognized merit. Besides, the goal of this work is to accredit the qualities and the virtues by which our little population is marked, especially in the gloomy times of slavery. A single stroke, if it is well executed, finds a large place here, that is why I place Mlle. Virginia Girodeau among our remarkable personalities whose glory is worthy of remembrance..."

The *Theatre de la Renaissance* was also used by the Colored Creole Philharmonic Society, organized in the 1830s. *L'Orchestre de la Societe Philharmonique*, for some time under the direction of M. Constatin Deburque, was the only Philharmonic Orchestra in the city and throughout the South in the 19th century.

Desdunes' history of the Louisiana Creole people does not tell us as much about the Creole musicians as we could wish, but his comments are interesting and worth quoting at some length:

"The Music of the Creoles"

"The Creole population of color produced excellent musicians and composers of superior merit. Among those whose talent commended particular attention, in Louisiana and even abroad, were the Lamberts, the father and two sons. The father, it is said, was the most accomplished of the three. Unfortunately he left us nothing, probably because Louisiana was insufficiently developed at that time to appreciate his musical genius.

But his sons were well received in Paris, Portugal and in Brazil. Lucien was the author of numerous compositions which he dedicated to the most distinguished personages of these different countries... The Lamberts shone for a long time in Louisiana, but as with so many others, they preferred to live elsewhere, where the conditions of life appeared more favorable to them than those which they encountered at the place of their birth. They were pianists and they played that instrument at the Orleans Theater.

Other artists took part in their concerts, among them the celebrated Gottshalk. Despite the changes since the war, those aware of certain details have not forgotten what happened at these artistic reunions. There existed a little artistic rivalry

84

between Gottshalk and Lambert, this was happily resolved by the ingenious intervention of common friends who gave to each one of these geniuses an equal part of the glory. Gottshalk was recognized as the master of Lambert as instrumentalist, and Lambert the master of Gottshalk as composer. At this time, in 1843, it was only a question of the respective merits of these two great musicians."

From these remarks of Desdunes it can be seen there is nothing very new or modern about cutting contests. Here we are told of a competition between white and colored musicians which took place in New Orleans in the mid-19th century. The date given, however, is in error, perhaps a misprint. Possibly Desdunes intended 1853 to be the date for this event.

Louis Moreau Gottshalk was born in New Orleans in 1829, the son of an immigrant father and a mother distantly related to the French aristocracy. A child prodigy, in 1842 he was sent to France to continue his education studying under the tutelage of Berlioz. While in France Gottshalk produced a number of his most famous compositions, and incidentally became an opponent of slavery. He returned to America in 1853, this being the probable date for his encounter with Lambert.

Some of Gottshalk's compositions written while he was still in Europe, particularly one entitled *Bamboula, Dance des Negres,* can be counted among the many reasons for the continuation of the Congo Square myth discussed earlier. Gottshalk undoubtably heard the story of the Congo Square dancers during his youth in New Orleans, although he could not have had any personal experience of them as he was born long after all such activity had been made illegal. In any event his later meeting with Lambert must have enlightened his view of Creole musical capabilities.

No recordings were possible in those days of course, so Gottshalk is known today not for his instrumental ability but as an excellent composer. It is interesting to note then, that in this long-ago battle of music, although the contestants were thought to be fairly evenly matched, Lambert the Creole was judged to be the better composer. An indication, surely, of the high quality of musicianship then prevalent among the Creole musicians of New Orleans.

To continue with Desdunes' observations of the 19th century musicians:

"Eugene Macarty"

"Mr. Eugene Macarty was an excellent pianist. He was more fortunate than his contemporaries because the public became interested in his personality and his compositions. Some even held that he was the only artist of merit among the Creoles. It is known however, from the reports of people worthy of faith and of an indubitable competence that Eugene Macarty was not even the equal of the Lamberts in the theory of music and still less in invention.

According to these reports the Lamberts produced more and better work than Macarty; but the latter was varied in his talents. This versatility was remarkable for it was always shown to his advantage on all occasions. Macarty had a baritone voice which was rich, sonorous and admirably cultivated...he was an actor by nature...In the stage enterprises organized by the Creole people Macarty filled the leading role by common consent...Macarty was also an orator. Gifted with a strong voice and a clear diction, his speech was smooth and eloquent. At the beginning of the Reconstruction Macarty often spoke to the people, discussing with force and intelligence questions of right and of liberty, he never failed to receive the warmest applause. It can be said that Macarty was a musician, singer, actor and politician."

"Samuel Snaer"

"Samuel Snaer was perhaps more knowledgeable in music than Macarty, but his modesty seriously hindered him. Although the violin was the instrument preferred by Snaer, it is nevertheless a fact that he played a dozen instruments with talent. Snaer had a fine tenor voice but he preferred not to sing. He mastered harmony but his compositions remained at the bottom of his trunk, where time and the insects waged war on them.

To the public Samuel Snaer only represented a very ordinary instrumentalist, but for the good judges who knew him intimately, he was a musical genius. Like Eugene Macarty, Samuel Snaer was a native of New Orleans. He was a very good organist; for a long time he was the organist of St. Mary's church on Chartres Street . . ."[9]

"Edmond Dede"

"Edmond Dede was a Black, born in New Orleans around 1829, contemporary of Macarty and Snaer. He is always spoken of as a prodigy on the violin. His first studies in New Orleans were under the direction of skilled and conscientious teachers. After mastering as much of the art that a man of his color could learn here, he went to Europe on the advise of sympathetic friends. He first visited Belgium but not having found the object of his search in this little realm, he went to Paris where he was welcomed with hospitality . . .

By the intervention of good friends he did not have to wait to be admitted to the Paris Conservatory of Music by audition. His progress and his triumphs quickly drew him to the attention of the musical world. From then on he enjoyed all the fame accorded to true merit. Dede later became the head of the orchestra at the Theater of Bordeaux, where for more than twenty-seven years he held the baton of director.

This artist came back to New Orleans in 1893 and gave several concerts where the connoisseurs could appreciate his high qualities . . . he had memorized the works of all the great masters . . . his own works were of an elevated order. He had even started the composition of a grand opera *Le Sultan d'Espanan* which he could not finish on account of illness. Edmond Dede died at Paris in 1903.

"Basil Barres"

"Here is a Creole of Color who was certainly very popular in New Orleans. French in heart and in spirit, he was an accomplished gentleman and everyone enjoyed knowing him. Basil Barres was born in our city; when still a young man he was employed by Mr. Perrier the great merchant of French music on Royal Street. He learned piano there and quickly became an artist of the first order.

Mr. Perrier sent him on several trips to Paris in the interest of his House. He always came back with the love of France grown greater in his heart. Mr. Barres was a piano tuner, a professor of music and a composer. His dance pieces were very popular in New Orleans. When the great violinist Dede stayed among us, it was Basil Barres whom he chose as his accompanist . . ."

It can be seen from Desdunes' remarks the Creole musicians did not draw any distinction between classical music and dance music. It was all simply music based on the same principles and merely adapted for different uses. Thus Barres, distinguished primarily for his dance music, was also the accompanist for Dede, who achieved eminence for his playing and composing of classical music. Desdunes makes it apparent that in the days long before the commercialized music of tin pan alley it was taken for granted a musician should not only be able to play music of all kinds but also be capable of composing all types of music.

The great popularity of dancing in New Orleans over a period of more than two centuries, at times amounting to a mild mania, was due in large part to the excellent dance music provided by the Creole musicians. It is appropriate then, to add a comment from 1895 by an unusually perceptive and courageous member of the white dancing convocation of New Orleans:

". . . as for the Creole music, it is quite permissible to say it in New Orleans, that no one has ever known the full poetry and inspiration of the dance who has not danced to the original music of a Macarty or a Basile Barès. [sic] And it is a pleasure to own the conviction, whether it can be maintained or not with reason, that America will one day do homage for music of a fine and original type to some representative of Louisiana's colored population."[10]

Under the Jim Crow segregation laws of that period southern whites had few good feelings for people of other races or colors. It is worth noting the writer of these prophetic words believed, or perhaps hoped, it was "permissible" for a white person to praise the Creole musicians and their "original music." After a long and distinguished career Macarty died in 1881. The "music of a fine and original type" therefore, must have been enjoyed by white audiences, to the knowledge of that author, for at least several decades before the 1890s.

Much of Desdunes' history has to do with the affairs of the Creoles in their fight for civil rights. This is interesting social history deserving of greater study, but here we are concerned only with the music of New Orleans. At this point then, we close the window of our Creole historian and go on to observe how Creole music underwent a process of continuing development.

Notes for Part II

1. This foreword to *Nos Hommes et Notre Histoire* (see note 8 below) is initialed "L. M."; Charles Barthelemy Rousseve, in his book *The Negro in Louisiana* (New Orleans: 1937. p. 23) attributes the foreword to "L. Martin, French Canadian. . ." Rousseve also notes (p. 39) the 23rd marriage recorded in the St. Louis Cathedral archives at New Orleans was between two Free People of Color, the man a trumpeter in Governor Bienville's army. This was in 1724, only six years after the founding of New Orleans.

2. Details of colonial law are available in the colonial records of the Cabildo at Louisiana State Museum library, New Orleans.

3. Acts of the Louisiana Legislature 1803–1860.

4. The French word *cassette*, meaning casket, became the Creole word casquet. Not to be confused with another French word *casquette*. At one time there was a Casquet street in New Orleans named in recognition of the casquet girls.

5. Grace King, *New Orleans; the Place and the People* (New York; Macmillan, 1895. 1915) p. 122.

6. Cabildo documents.

7. Grace King. Ibid. p. 266.

8. Rodolphe L. Desdunes, *Nos Hommes et Notre Histoire* (Montreal: Arbour and Dupont, 1911) trans. Jane Julian. *Our Men and Our Story. Homage to the Creole Population, In Remembrance of the Great Men it Produced and the Good Deeds it Accomplished.*

9 Albert Snaer, a trumpet player believed to have been a member of the Samuel Snaer family, recorded with the Dewey Jackson Orchestra in 1928, and in the 1930s with the Claude Hopkins Orchestra.

10 Grace King. Ibid. p. 338.

PART III

THE EARLY DEVELOPMENT

CHAPTER 10

THE DANCE HALLS

Although New Orleans Creole musicians were equally well qualified to play all the various categories of music it was inevitable they would specialize in dance music. There was a limited demand for classical and operatic music in the city. There was almost no market for music of any sort throughout the remainder of what was then a cultureless South based upon the degradation of human beings through the system of slavery. But with its Creole-French legacy there was an enthusiastic and continuing demand for dance music in New Orleans.

Until the mid-19th century however, dance music in New Orleans, as elsewhere, was provided by string bands. Bands composed entirely of stringed instruments. The instrumentation of these bands varied, usually there were violins, violas, mandolins and guitars. There were no drums or banjos. Those instruments were in existance but were thought to be unsuitable for string bands.

Larger stringed instruments such as bass fiddle, 'cello or piano were used only on those jobs that had the space and the facilities.

The neighborhood dance halls built by the Creole and other local social clubs gave evidence in their construction as to the size of the early string bands. Dozens of these dance halls were built in New Orleans during the 19th century but it is doubtful if any two halls had exactly the same design. Some had the bandstand positioned at the front of the hall, some at the rear, a few on the side. Uptown halls, built at a later period, had low bandstands varying in height from one foot to about five feet above the dance floor, not very different from the modern bandstands. The older downtown halls had stands that were really balconies, sometimes called galleries, ten to fourteen feet high.

The *Francs Amis* (Free Friends) society is thought to have been one of the earliest of the downtown Creole societies. Certainly it was in existence before 1845 when the song writer Nichol Ricquet wrote a *Rondeau Redoubler* dedicated to the *Francs Amis* and subsequently published in *Les Cenelles*. It is believed the society became dormant during the worst of the slave system oppression. In 1860, with the imminence of the Civil War, the association was reactivated and their hall became one of the most active dance halls of the Reconstruction period. Many of the Creoles who attained responsible positions in the Reconstruction governments of Louisiana held their social events in this hall including the Lieutenant Governors P. B. S. Pinchback and H. C. C. Antoine.

The design of the *Francs Amis* Hall followed the same pattern as the 18th century dance halls of France. It was sturdily constructed of cypress wood, still well preserved and in use as a church in the mid-20th century. The floor space measured about one hundred feet long by forty feet wide but from the musicians standpoint it was extremly cramped. In those days musicians were considered only as the hired help and little attention was paid to their comfort. The bandstand consisted of a balcony three and a half feet wide by twenty feet long projecting from the front wall of the dance floor, about twelve feet high.

Access to the balcony was difficult to obtain. Upon entering the hall a short passageway led to the dance floor. In the side of this passage there was a narrow door which opened to a steep flight of stairs barely eighteen inches wide. These steps ascended to what can only be described as a loft under the naked rafters of the roof. From the loft, entrance to the balcony was made by way of a sliding window panel less than four feet in height. The balcony was just wide enough for a man to sit in a straight-backed chair and was enclosed by a balustrade some three feet high. The balustrade rail also served as the music stand, consisting of a sloping board upon which the sheet music could be placed. It is evident that it would have been difficult to take any instrument bigger than a guitar up to the balcony, nor was there sufficient elbowroom on the balcony for a larger instrument to be played. The whole situation was so confining we can be sure no stout musicians ever played there.

94

Francs Amis (Free Friends) Hall.

The band balcony at Francs Amis Hall.

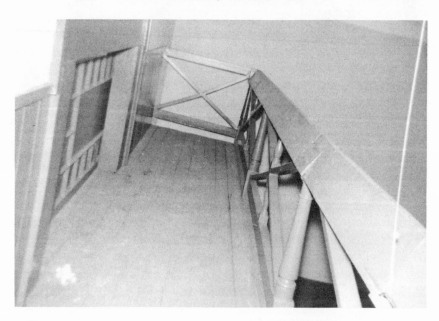

View on the narrow band balcony at Francs Amis Hall. On the right is the sloping rail that served as the music stand; the sliding access panel is on the left.

The length of the balcony indicates these were small bands, there was space for only half a dozen musicians and obviously they were all seated in a straight line. There was no place for the leader to be out in front where he could be seen and where he could conduct the band. Therefore a method had to be devised to keep the band playing as a unit.

Foot stomping became the answer.

It is commonplace now for the leader to "stomp off" a band even when standing in full view, but the development of the foot stomp came about precisely because the leader could not be observed by the band. Band balconies did not have a rigid support under them, they were constructed on beams that projected out from the wall. For this reason they transmitted any vibration very distinctly. It was the vibration as much as the sound of the foot stomp which kept the band playing together as a unit. In a noisy hall with perhaps hundreds of people milling around, the sound of the foot stomp was not always to be heard but the vibration of the balcony was unmistakable. Again, the signal for the last or "out" chorus could be felt even if the sound was not heard above the music.

Stomp signals do not appear to have changed over the many decades since they were first developed by the New Orleans musicians. They are simple but remarkably efficient. One stomp is similar to a conductor raising his baton. It means "get ready." The next several stomps determine the tempo of the number and the beat on which to start. After the number has been played for a suitable period of time the final stomp, at the beginning of what will be the last chorus, enables the band to know when to stop playing or to "go out" together.

The significance of the stomp-off is most apparent when for some reason it does not operate properly. For an example let us cite a typically impromptu New Orleans recording session which took place in a studio carpeted by a thick rug. In order to use separate microphones for each instrument the members of the band were widely spaced. The leader was positioned in such a way that he could not be easily observed by the other members of the band. When all was made ready the director retired to the recording booth and made a sign to the leader to start the session. Accordingly the leader gave the customary stomp-off and began playing. He was surprised to find he was playing solo. In the confusion of events it had been overlooked that a thick rug is an unsuitable surface to convey stomp signals.

The Tuxedo was a cabaret in the red-light district of New Orleans which will be discussed more fully later. Built in 1911, it was arranged in the customary style of a New Orleans cabaret with chairs and tables along the sides of the dance floor and in front of the band. The bandstand was of the platform type, four feet high and solidly constructed. The band was arranged across the platform with the piano, played by the leader Manuel Manetta, angled out from the wall. With that arrangement the band complained they could not see, hear or feel the stomp-off. Manetta solved the problem in a practical manner typical of New Orleans musicians. He sawed a length off the kitchen mop handle, to the chagrin of his wife, and took it to the Tuxedo. Seated at the piano the handle fitted comfortably between his knees and did not impede his playing. With the shortened mop handle he was able to strike the floor with loud hammer-like thumps which were unmistakable. Manetta humorously referred to this as the "knock-off", certainly it was not the conventional stomp-off. But perhaps it would be incorrect to call it a mop-off.

In the dance halls of New Orleans there was no "front line" of musicians or a rhythm section at the rear. There was only one straight line of musicians. The instruments, however, were not seated at random. Traditionally the straight line always had the lead instruments in the center with the harmony and rhythm instruments positioned at each end of the line. There was a double purpose to this plan. Since the leader was usually a violinist playing the straight lead parts, he was seated in the center so the melody was always audible to the band. The arrangement also achieved a balance of sound.

The modern New Orleans dance band, of course, is no longer a string band, but the tradition tends to linger on. An experiment was tried at another recording session in New Orleans. This one was on a stage in an auditorium. The chairs for the band were placed in a straight line across the stage. When the musicians arrived they first sat in the nearest available chair. When no one intervened they began to rearrange themselves, saying "I should be here, you should be there", until the traditional alignment of instruments was attained. This is remarkable when it is kept in mind that for decades New Orleans musicians have been accustomed to playing on modern square, round, or irregularly shaped bandstands or at sessions that did not allow for the traditional straight line.

The most famous of the 19th century New Orleans dance halls was the Orleans Ballroom. It was built by John Davis, born in Paris in 1773. He arrived in New Orleans in 1809, eventually to become the most noted impresario of his time. The Orleans Ballroom opened in 1817. Most probably Davis would have designed the interior structure in the French style, but with only one exception no descriptions of it have been discovered. After more than sixty years of use the ballroom was offered for sale in 1881. It was purchased by Thomy Lafon, the wealthy Creole philanthropist, who then presented it to the colored sisters of the Society of the Holy Family to be used as their chapel. This is not an unusual fate for old dance halls in New Orleans, several of which were converted into churches as the Gallic traditions of the city gradually faded from memory.

It is from this period, the late 19th century after the building had ended its days as a dance hall, that we get our single brief description of the interior. When conducting a guest on a tour of the Convent a sister of the Order is quoted, in 1895, as follows:

"This", said the sister, stopping at the chapel door, "is the old Orleans ballroom; they say it is the best dancing floor in the world. It is made of three thicknesses of cypress. That is the balcony where the ladies and gentlemen used to promenade . . ."[1]

The good sister not being familiar with dance halls evidently was confused by the presence of the balcony, misinterpreting its use. The "ladies and gentlemen" did their promenading on the dance floor, not the balcony. That was reserved for the musicians.

The existence of a balcony in a dance hall built by a Frenchman only a few years after the colonial occupation ended, dates this type of construction as the earliest style. Although the description of the Orleans Ballroom is admittedly meager it does illustrate the two most prominent features of the early dance halls. They had good dance floors, for it is much less tiring to dance on a good floor, and the bandstands were not stands in the usual sense of the word, they were balconies. Those dance halls that had the best floor and the best music would be the ones that did the most business.

Dance floors were waxed in a very practical manner. Before a dance took place fine shavings of candle wax were distributed on the surface. In the course of the evening these shavings were then literally danced into the floor. This procedure was very effective. After the *Francs Amis* Hall had been used as a church for several decades the floor still had a glass-like shine from the many coats of wax that had been deposited on it and danced into it.

One further point should be made to the purpose of the band-balconies. In the early days musicians were regarded as a necessary but alien presence in the hall. Possibly this attitude was a holdover from the balls at the Versailles Court where the musicians were the only persons present who were not members of the aristocracy. Some Creole societies were also notably exclusive, referred to as "dicty" or snooty by the musicians. At the *Francs Amis* Hall musicians who were not Creoles were not allowed to leave the balcony or loft area, as several of the older musicians have recalled. Even as late as the 1950s non-Creoles were similarly restricted to the bandstand at a few of the Creole social affairs as the author can personally attest. At the 19th century slave society balls of the white folks, assuredly Creole musicians would have been prohibited from leaving their allotted work space. Given this social attitude it is evident that putting the musicians on a balcony not only conserved room for the dancers, it permitted the dancers to concentrate on the sound of the music without the "distraction" of observing those who were creating that sound.

This did not protect the musicians from criticism. In reporting the Mardi Gras balls of 1858 the *Daily Delta* newspaper said:

"The principle attraction in the Terpsichorean line was the Young Men's Ball at Odd Fellows Hall where Monsieur Musard discoursed fine music from the gallery notwithstanding he was hissed terribly at one time by a company of Lancers for making a mistake in the figures..."[2]

Perhaps it was fortunate M. Musard was on the balcony, or the gallery as it is called here, where he was safe from physical assault after bungling a lancers' quadrille dance.

The type of dance hall we have been discussing might be termed the early balcony style. There were several other general types of dance halls built in downtown New Orleans at various periods during the 19th century. Small neighborhood halls such as the *Juenes Amis* (Young Friends) and the *Artisan* societies were built on an area roughly corresponding to a housing lot. The early style, as at Artisan Hall, had small cramped balconies. But the halls built at a later period, such as the *Juenes Amis*, had elevated platforms. These platforms were lower, only six to eight feet high, with steps leading directly off the dance floor. From the musicians' point of view the later platform type was an improvement because they were considerably wider, being supported by a rigid framework.

Another type of dance hall was the two-storied building, a style favored by the white societies and masonic lodges. In these halls the dance floor was usually on the upper story leaving the ground floor available for offices, meeting rooms and other business enterprises. The most interesting of the two story halls built for the colored organizations was the one built for the Friends of Hope society, popularly known as Hope's or Hope Hall. This large building in the heart of the old Creole section later was managed by a co-operative and then became known as Co-operator's Hall. There were two Hope Halls; the first one also contained a restaurant as we see from this 1856 report:

"Hope Hall"
"This pleasant and well-managed restaurant is one of the most quiet, snug and satisfactory to get a dinner and lunch or a rare dish to be found in any city. There is a novelty in the arrangement of the little private dinner stalls which give an unusually pleasant aspect to the place..."[3]

The second hall was built in 1888, apparently on the same site, and opened with a Fancy Dress and Calico Ball in February 1889. Two months later it was reported the Promise Social Club

The Hall of the Jeunes Amis (Young Friends) Society.

The band platform at Jeunes Amis Hall.

On the band platform at Jeunes Amis Hall the pipes for gaslight were still in place.

A memorial plaque to Thomy Lafon at Jeunes Amis Hall.

also used the hall, holding a Parade and Ball with a band of fourteen pieces.[4]

Hope's Hall was well designed. From the ground floor wide stairways on each side led to a large dance floor made of rectangular cypress blocks arranged in a herringbone pattern, still in good condition in the 1950s after many years of use and several decades of disuse. The accommodation for the band represented a curious transition between the balcony and the platform style. Situated at the front of the hall it was as high as a balcony, fourteen feet above the dance floor with another eight feet of headroom to the ceiling and faced by a sturdy balustrade. Underneath, however, it was enclosed and supported in the manner of a platform. The stairs leading to the bandstand, protected by a small gate, were arranged in two flights. These were not the narrow almost secretive stairs of earlier dance halls. They were openly visible and led directly off the dance floor. Moreover, the steps were three feet in width, sufficiently wide to accommodate large musical instruments.

The top of the stairs opened onto a huge bandstand, astonishing in its size, really more a stage than a stand. It stretched the full width of the hall, about forty feet, and extended more than twenty feet from front to back. The rear of this immense backstand area was probably used as the space for the musicians to take their rest period as it was so high they could not be observed from the dance floor.

This spacious hybrid, a cross between a platform, a balcony and a stage, was one of the largest of its type ever built in New Orleans. Clearly this was not a bandstand intended for small string bands. It was constructed so as to be suitable for bands composed of many musicians, some of them playing bulky instruments. In brief, the bandstand at Hope's Hall was specifically designed to accommodate large brass bands.

There can be no doubt brass bands did play regularly in Hope's Hall. Older residents of the neighborhood could remember such events still occurring as late as the 1920s after it had become known as Co-Operator's Hall. It has long been the practice in New Orleans for brass bands to play for a parade and then play for the dance that often follows, these affairs were common in the 1950s. Hope's Hall appears to have been constructed especially for the brass band 'Parade and Dance' event.

Perhaps the most renowned 19th century downtown dance hall for colored people was Globe Hall. There are occasional newspaper references to this hall during the slavery years. It too was capacious, a two story structure able to accommodate large bands. The hall was demolished in the 1920s but the interior design was remembered as being somewhat similar to Hope's Hall.

A study of the design of early downtown New Orleans dance halls and their bandstands make it possible to picture the type of bands that were used for dancing at the time of their construction. Thus the balconies of the earliest halls were suitable only for small string bands. At a later date the smaller halls were built with platforms that had sufficient space for larger bands. And the biggest halls had the capacity to comfortably accommodate large brass bands.

The Hall of the Friends of Hope Society. Later known as Co-operators Hall.

The head of stairs on the spacious band platform at Hope's Hall.

The Hall of the Economy Society.

CHAPTER 11

THE BRASS BANDS

The history of the New Orleans brass bands has been largely ignored by jazz historians for the reason that there is no way to reconcile the existence of brass bands in early New Orleans with the conventional histories of jazz. At the time when slaves were brought to America the African people had no brass bands or anything remotely resembling them. Brass musical instruments are a product of modern industry, they cannot be produced by non-industrial societies in Africa or elsewhere. Consequently, with few exceptions, advocates of the African origin theory have paid little attention to the brass bands of New Orleans. The history of such bands has been ignored also by those who support theories of invention since brass band music was not invented in New Orleans nor even in America. Those who recommend evolutionary theories have been similarly perplexed because it is not clear to them how jazz music could have evolved from brass band music. Jazz history books would have us believe early jazz bands such as that of Bolden were influenced by mythical late 19th century Congo Square dancers but not at all affected by the music of the brass bands very much in evidence throughout the city. An illogical idea plainly contrary to common sense.

New Orleans musicians played all kinds of music. They drew no distinction between dance music, classical music or any other kind of music including marching music. They specialized in dance music because that was their primary means of obtaining employment. With the advent of reliable brass instruments during the first half of the 19th century another avenue for earning a living from music became available and many of the string instrument musicians began to play brass instruments or to double in brass.

Conventional histories of New Orleans jazz usually assume there were no brass bands in the city before the Civil War. Repeatedly it is asserted the tradition of the brass bands commenced because of the availability of military brass band instruments in New Orleans pawn shops when the war ended. This sounds plausible until it is examined in the light of historical facts.

Three years before the end of the Civil War New Orleans was occupied by Union troops under the command of General Butler. Martial law was established in the city on May 1, 1862 and any equipment not removed by the Confederate armed forces was immediately confiscated. In view of the fact that Union troops remained in New Orleans for several years it is highly unlikely that any musical instruments belonging to either the Confederate or Union armies would have been allowed to find their way into the city's pawn shops. Nor would that have been necessary; New Orleans never suffered from a lack of musical instruments.

The Creoles were not a poverty stricken class of people, music was in such great demand during the 19th century that Creole musicians were able to make a good living. They would not have been dependent upon cast-off military supplies. France had been supplying the city's music trade for many years. French instruments manufactured to suit the pitch requirement of the 19th century could still be found in the city as late as the 1950s even though businesses in the music trade routinely destroy most of the old instruments traded in for new ones.

There is additional evidence to be observed in the larger neighborhood dance halls designed to suit brass bands, they would not have been built unless it had already been shown there was a market for dance music played by brass bands. That market was realized by the famous "second line" of street dancers which traditionally followed the brass band parades for the numerous social organizations of the city. It was reasoned that if people could dance to brass band music in the streets they could also do so in dance halls.

Led by professional Creole brass bands, parades were common in Ante-Bellum New Orleans although, as with the Creole

111

dance bands and other aspects of Creole culture, little evidence of their activities was allowed to appear in print. There were occasional notices however, from which we may draw inferences. For example on December 8, 1852 Mayor A. B. Crossman declared a public holiday to commemorate the deaths of three famous southern politicians—John C. Calhoun, Henry Clay and Daniel Webster. A symbolic funeral procession was staged in which the military, the fire department and "benevolent and other societies" were invited to participate. The *Picayune* newspaper issued a pamphlet in recognition of "the public demonstration of grief" in which it reported "the wailing funeral notes of many bands". Cited in particular were the Field Band of the Washington Regiment and two bands of the Louisiana Legion. But there were also four other musical aggregations which were alluded to merely as "bands of music", the method commonly used to describe the Creole bands. After the ceremonies were concluded "the different societies and corps, civil and military, then moved out of the square to the sound of gay music and the crowds began to disperse."[5]

The significance of this reference to gay music after a funeral parade will be seen later. For the moment it is worth noting that gay music was scarcely to be expected from mid-19th century military bands. Dirges and funeral marches were undoubtedly part of their repertoire, but the function of the military bands of that time was to play martial music suitable for marching soldiers. It is improbable that the bands of the Washington Regiment or the Louisiana Legion would have played music which could be described as gay. From the Creole bands however, gay or lively music now called jazz, is exactly what could have been expected.

Another mention of a New Orleans Ante-Bellum parade was this newspaper report of 1856:

"The Portuguese Benevolent Society"

"This array of charity exhibited its strength as proposed, in our streets on the occasion of its annual anniversary. With inspiriting music and gay banners, the procession moved

The ceremonial hearse used at the symbolic funeral for Clay, Calhoun and Webster. 1852.

The Hall of the Portuguese Lusitanos Society.

Canal street, dividing New Orleans, as it looked in the mid-19th century.

through the city attracting the favorable notice of thousands . . ."6

As usual in the scarce reports of that period there is no indication of just who was providing the "inspiriting music." There should be little doubt in our minds these were bands of professional Creole musicians.

The Portuguese Society was probably the first of the city's minority associations, this report unfortunately does not tell us how many annual anniversaries the society was celebrating in 1856. It is believed the origin of the group, also known as the Lusitanos Society, extended back to the colonial period. Their headquarters were housed in a two storied brick building the exterior architecture of which was identical to the Spanish buildings of the old town. It was located downriver at the corner of Champs Elysee and Rue Dauphine, just outside what was then the city limit of the Spanish colony. During the 1930s the building was converted for residential and commercial use obliterating the original interior design. Musicians who played there in the 1920s have recalled the Lusitania Dance Hall, as it was commonly called, was on the second floor but details of the interior are unclear. As an early minority group the Portuguese may have felt an affinity for the Creoles. Colored bands played for their social affairs throughout the existence of the society until it disbanded with the onset of the 1930s depression.

Because of the social mores prevalent before the Civil War we should not expect Creole brass bands to be mentioned by name in print any more than we could expect to hear of Creole dance bands. The very fact they are not specifically described in these scanty newspaper reports is really all the evidence needed to infer they would be the professional bands of the colored Creoles.

In the 19th century before the inception of Trade Unions and Insurance companies there were many Social, Benevolent or "Aid and Pleasure" organizations in New Orleans for both white and colored people. For example before the Laborers Union was formed the *Daily Delta* for March 10, 1859 reported a parade of that Union's predecessor:

"United Laborers Benevolent Society"

"This society was out in procession this morning with their beautiful banner and flags, and accompanied by several bands of music . . ."[7]

Again the "bands of music" are anonymous and again we may be sure they would be the professional Creole brass bands hired for the occasion by the Laborers Society. It is worth noting there was no shortage of these pre-Civil War brass bands as several could be used for one parade.

The population of 19th century New Orleans was divided in many ways besides those involving race or the slavery condition. Social groups were formed in which the members all had something in common—their trade or profession, their nationality, language or immigrant status. At first these groups were small and their social affairs were confined to local dances for which the traditional small string band was sufficient. A few dance halls could be made to serve the needs of several social clubs by renting out the hall. Frequently the halls would be rented for every night of the week. It soon became apparent that owning a dance hall could be a very profitable investment.

As the population of New Orleans rapidly expanded and prospered the number, size and prosperity of the local social organizations also grew. Each group eager to build its own combination dance hall and lodge headquarters. "Social Aid and Pleasure" societies proliferated throughout the city.

A number of procedures were employed by these associations to raise funds which could then be used for benevolent work or perhaps to finance the building of a dance hall. One method was to parade through the streets with banners flying advertising their group, hoping in this manner to increase their membership. This could be made financially more rewarding by promoting a dance at the conclusion of the parade. An admission price could be charged or donations solicited from those parade followers and street dancers forming the "second line" who wished to continue their pleasure inside the dance hall. Once the dance was in progress it was possible to realize a small profit by providing refreshments.

Sometimes there was a problem in fitting a brass band into the older dance halls built to accomodate the string bands of an earlier time. The small balconies were useless for a large brass band. In these halls the band simply used part of the dance floor as their bandstand. For many years the bandstand-balcony at Artisan Hall was the subject of local humor. Here the problem was not only the small size of the balcony but also its height. Because of the low ceiling there was relatively little headroom for the band.

When the bands began to change from the arm-cradled bass horn to the over-the-shoulder tuba, the ceiling was found to be too low for the bell of the instrument even though the bass player was seated. The problem was solved in a typically pragmatic fashion by cutting a hole in the ceiling. The resulting opening was then fitted with a panel that could be removed when necessary. This solution was not entirely satisfactory from the bass player's point of view. He had to sit in exactly the right place so the bell of the tuba projected through the opening, and he had to be careful not to move around too much for a collision of the bell with the ceiling could result in a lip bruise. Sitting in one position without being able to occasionally adjust is a tiring experience which did not endear tuba players to Artisan Hall.

Parades were sponsored in part by local retailers. The parading lodge or society halted at pre-arranged rest stops along the route. Convenient barrooms and restaurants serving as oases where the thirsty paraders and second liners could purchase refreshments enabling them to continue their parading and dancing endeavors, increasing the volume of trade for those sponsoring businesses.

In the summer months many societies widened the scope of their activities to include outdoor events. Picnics were held in local parks and a parade through the streets would lead to the picnic grounds. Here again no picnic would be considered a success without dancing, for which donations were solicited and refreshments made available.

In later years, especially after Emancipation, day-long and weekend excursions were arranged for recreational areas along the shores of Lake Ponchartrain or vacation resorts on the Gulf Coast. For these open air activities the traditional string band

Artisan's Hall. Photo courtesy Bill Russell.

BARONNE ST., CORNER OF PERDIDO.
3 BLOCKS ONLY FROM CANAL ST.

FOR RENT BY THE DAY OR NIGHT.
SEATING CAPACITY 1,500. FINE ACOUSTICS, ETC.
Apply to P. WERLEIN,
CANAL STREET.   NEW ORLEANS, L

In the 1880s, featuring "fine acoustics" Werlein Hall was the largest of the uptown halls.

was inadequate. Playing music outdoors required a volume of sound beyond its capability. The brass band became as indispensable to the enthusiastic dancing population of New Orleans as the string bands had been in earlier times. Not that the string band was entirely replaced, there still were many occasions for dancing where the small string band was considered preferable and both types of bands co-existed peacefully in the city.

With the arrival of the brass bands an event occurred which subsequently was to have enormous influence with jazz theoreticians and historians. For the first time, a century after dance bands became popular, drums appeared in New Orleans dance halls and people danced to music that included a drum beat. But the drums did not appear from African sources. They arrived as an integral part of the brass band.

Brass musical instruments are a product of the industrial revolution. The origin of drums in New Orleans dance music therefore, has a line of ancestry that stems not from African music but from the modern brass band! As part of the normal instrumentation of the brass bands, however, there would not have been one man playing a set of drums, that innovation had yet to be developed. These were orthodox brass bands with one man allotted for the snare drum and another man for the bass drum.

Parades and dances were not the only functions of the brass bands. The famous music funerals of New Orleans also formed an important part of their duties.

In the 1890s New Orleans began a method of draining the city by means of a pumping system. Before that time the water table had been only a few inches below ground level. Under the circumstances, in the 18th and 19th centuries it was impracticable to inter the dead in the earth so tombs were constructed above ground as burial chambers to receive the deceased.

The accumulation of a tomb fund was one of the first objectives of the various social organizations of New Orleans. The aim was to obtain sufficient funds to build large multi-chambered mausoleums for the interment of their deceased members. Many of these tombs can still be seen in the old cemeteries of the city. A number of them are still in use. The records of the Girod street cemetery serve as an indication of how many social groups, at one time or another, have been in existence in the city. This one cemetery, in use from 1822 to 1957, contained several hundreds of these tombs including more than a hundred built and owned by various societies of colored people.[8]

When brass bands became available they were pressed into service to play dirges for the funeral processions of these societies as a mark of respect for the departed member. The New Orleans custom of providing funerals accompanied by brass bands has a tradition that extends back to a period before the Civil War, evinced by this newspaper notice from 1856 concerning our friends of the Portuguese Lusitanos society:

"Funeral Ceremonies"

"The funeral rites were performed on Saturday afternoon for Mr. J. B. Mueller and Charles bled, by the Portuguese Benevolent Association. The band which led the procession performed the most exquisite pieces of music and the members of the association turned out in considerable force."[9]

This band would almost certainly be the same one that played for the parades of the Portuguese Association. Societies tended to contract with the same bands year after year as long as their performance was satisfactory. Here the band is described as playing "exquisite pieces of music," probably hymns and dirges. The same type of music which was still being performed at New Orleans funerals a century later; whereas for the parades, as we have seen, their music was described as gay and inspiriting, or a type of music that would later be called jazz.

The question of the type of music played at New Orleans funerals has perplexed jazz historians for many years. How could these jazz musicians play dirges from written music? Play them *larghissimo*, so slowly that they become extremely difficult to play properly; and then play the "best jazz in the world" as some writers have termed it, on the return from the cemetery? The presumption is that New Orleans musicians are not able to read music but even if they could, surely they would not be able to play dirges in such a professional manner. And why would they play jazz music at a funeral? The confusion arises because the subject has been inadequately researched and not fully considered from the viewpoint of the participants, particularly the musicians.

When a band contracts for a parade or a funeral there is always a stipulated time and place for the assembly of the band. The place may be anywhere close to the job, usually a convenient corner bar is selected. The time is always one hour before the job is due to start. This allows time for any late-comers to arrive and also provides a few moments to obtain refreshments and to greet friends of the neighborhood before the work commences. The band then lines up and marches in an orderly manner to the place where the employment will begin, usually the headquarters, lodge or hall of a society. A bright marching pace is set by the snare drum at about ninety to one-hundred beats, or steps, per minute. The band plays a warm-up parade tune on the way so their arrival on the job is self-announced. Here the members of the lodge, with their banners prominently displayed, form into ranks behind the band. A parade marshal leads the procession along the chosen route, the band follows him and the parade begins.

If this is a funeral procession the snares are released from the drum or perhaps muffled by the simple expedient of stuffing a handkerchief between the snares and the drumhead. With banners furled the procession goes to the funeral establishment, church or home of the deceased with the band playing hymns at march tempo. At this point the funeral cortege with the hearse joins the procession and the band, in New Orleans terminology, is said to have "picked up the body." If the funeral rites have been performed the procession goes directly to the cemetery, if not, the cortege goes first to the church where the band waits until the ceremonies conclude, it then proceeds to the cemetery.

Only dirges are played as long as the hearse remains with the procession interspersed with march tempo cadences marked with single beats of the muffled drum. Dirges are played at an excruciatingly slow tempo, as slow as twenty beats per minute. A long roll on the muffled snare drum introduces the beat

123

which is set by the bass drum. At this painfully slow pace it is necessary to know not only how to play properly but also how to walk as the step is taken only on the first beat of each bar. With such a long pause between steps the stride is executed in half-steps to avoid being constantly off balance. These half-steps cause the band to sway slowly from side to side in unison as the balance of weight slowly changes from one foot to the other. The total display of the slow pace, the mournful dirge and the swaying back and forth leaves a deep impression of solemnity. It is all done in a very professional manner. At this stage of the proceedings the band is said to be "carrying the body."

The hearse is often escorted to the burial site provided it is in an older cemetery situated close to the city. Here the band will play another dirge as the casket is interred. If the destination is a distant cemetery the band escorts the hearse for several blocks. The procession then divides into two lines. This enables the funeral cortege, accompanied by the family and mourners of the society, to proceed between the ranks. To the sound of the funeral dirge the cortege then continues on unescorted.

With no disrespect intended this operation is termed "turning the body loose" which simply means the funeral cortege has become separated from the procession. The phrase is part of the special vocabulary or jargon used by the journeymen of an ancient craft—that of New Orleans musician. These expressions represent certain stages or points of reference in the traditional procedure of the New Orleans brass band funeral.

This formality marks the end of the funeral but the work has not yet ended for the band. The final part of the job consists of escorting the procession of lodge members back to their headquarters. In gaining an understanding of what happens next it needs to be emphasized that the procession has become disassociated from the funeral; in effect it has been transformed into a normal parade similar in all respects to any other parade of local New Orleans societies. The lodge members again form ranks in their original order either at the place of leaving the cortege or outside the cemetery gates. The snare drummer replaces the snares on the drum head so the drum is no longer muffled. When all is ready the parade sets off to a lively marching beat of the snare drum. Soon the band will begin to play.

This is the point at which inexperienced parade watchers have proclaimed their astonishment that jazz should be played at a New Orleans funeral.

A jazz funeral!

There are two things wrong with this notion—the word jazz and the word funeral. It is a fallacy which discloses an unfamiliarity of the traditions of New Orleans societies and the brass band music of the city.

In the first place, at this stage of the proceedings the funeral has ended and the cortege has departed from the procession. It would be clearly unsuitable to continue to play slow dirges. The task before the band is to march the members of the society back to the dispersal site at their hall or lodge. Secondly, the band is not playing jazz, it is playing normal New Orleans parade music. Marching music in the New Orleans style.

Admittedly the parade music of a New Orleans brass band is unlike any other. It is nonetheless parade music, exactly the same music played at any other New Orleans parade. The only variance, which is not really a difference, is a concession to tradition. When it is thought to be appropriate the band will play *Oh Lady Be Good*, a tune added to the repertoire of the brass bands during the 1930s and dedicated, with typical New Orleans good humor, to an attractive widow. An older traditional tune *Oh Didn't He Ramble*, sometimes played as a six-eight march, was intended as a tribute to a ˙man thought to have lived a full life. Invariably on these occasions the band plays hymns in march tempo; *Just A Little While To Stay Here, In The Sweet Bye And Bye, Over In The Gloryland* and other traditional hymns.

In the past *When The Saints Go Marching In* was played regularly but when the hymn became degraded with improper use by dixieland bands it was quietly removed from the repertoire of the brass bands. An indication in itself that jazz is not played on these occasions and that the brass bands did not, and if they have a choice, will not play music considered to be jazz.

All of these tunes and hymns are used as regular parade marches played in 2/4, 4/4 or 6/8 time, at about 100 M. or steps per minute. None of them are exclusive to the aftermath of a funeral and none of them are jazz although, of course, they can be subjected to the jazz treatment by dixieland bands. At funerals the astonishing contrast between the extremely slow, deliberate music of the dirge and the bright tempo of the march has caused the neophyte parade watcher to believe New Orleans brass bands are playing jazz. Both types of music, the dirge and the march, are equally well executed but are clearly intended for quite different purposes.

The routine of brass band funerals is very ancient. Probably it has not changed appreciably since the mid-19th century. A downtown resident's brief description of a brass band funeral in the 1880s would have been entirely suitable for a similar funeral of the 1950s:

"Salle De L'Equity"

"This hall for colored people was located on our block. It was the meeting place for its members and rented also for balls, fairs, etc.

When there was a death of one of the members they would all meet there at the hall and accompanied by a band would march to the home of the deceased, playing on leaving, doleful music; it was very gloomy and weird. But on the return to the hall after the funeral the band was very joyful and played gay and loud music—then they would disband."[10]

Many of the New Orleans musicians developed a great fondness for the playing of dirges New Orleans style, taking pride in being able to master the difficult technique. Willie Pajeaud, trumpet player with the Eureka Brass Band, sometimes laughingly said he would rather play funeral dirges than eat. A sentiment with which many of the older New Orleans musicians would agree, revealing the pride skilled artisans take in a difficult task well done. A basic precept of the musicians is to create beauty in music. The dirges played at funerals reflect this attitude, they are skillfully executed and the style is unique. The New Orleans style applies to all types of music.

As with brass bands everywhere, the number and type of instruments used in the New Orleans bands changed over the course of time. Bands with all brass instruments have not been used for many years and generally speaking the 19th century brass bands were larger. To some degree the size of a band depended upon how much money the employing society was prepared to pay. Bands could vary from twelve to twenty pieces or even more on special occasions, the number of instruments could be augmented or decreased according to how large a band was needed for the job. In the 1880s a typical band probably had some nineteen musicians as can be inferred from this newspaper notice of 1882:

"The Grand United Order of Oddfellows in Louisiana will celebrate their 10th Anniversary on Wednesday 10th of May, by a grand parade in dress regalia through the principle streets and a promenade concert...Two bands of music, 38 musicians are engaged...."[11]

After the 1920s ten pieces gradually became the standard number of instruments for New Orleans brass bands, particularly after local 496 of the Musicians Union was formed in the city.[12]

The ten instruments consist of three trumpets, designated as lead, relief and solo; two trombones; two saxophones or one sax and one clarinet; one bass horn and two drums. The marching formation is arranged in four ranks. The two trombones and the bass horn lead the band in the first rank, the reed instruments form the second rank followed by the three trumpets and the drums. Although this is a small band, New Orleans musicians generate as large a volume of sound as bands of three or four times their size elsewhere, a source of some pride for New Orleans brass band musicians.

The most famous event involving brass bands are the Mardi Gras (literally, Fat Tuesday) or Shrove Tuesday parades, but these are not part of the tradition we have been discussing. With the exception of the Zulu's parade—a deliberate parody—for more than a hundred years Mardi Gras has been a white-dominated celebration. It has had little or no part in either the origin or the development of New Orleans music.

An early notice of New Orleans Mardi Gras was this (American) newspaper report of 1838:

"Shrove Tuesday"

"Today being the festival known by the above title (or Mardi Gras as the French call it) a number of ceremonies will be observed by a portion of our citizens preparatory to the beginning of Lent. The Carnival being at an end, a grand blowout will take place tonight with masquerade balls, cowbellions, etc."[13]

The Americans did not celebrate Mardi Gras at this time, only the French "portion of our citizens" were involved with balls and what the American newspaper contemptuously called "cowbellions" (cotillions). This is a clear indication of the churlish posture of early Anglo-American slavers for the Creole-French traditions of Louisiana. An indication also of the attitude of the slave society toward what they termed the "nigger music" of New Orleans.

By 1853, although there were still some Creole balls, the daytime celebrations of Mardi Gras had dwindled almost out of existence, as the *Daily True Delta* noted:

"Few and plebeian were the masquers who participated in the sports of this celebrated day of fun and fatness, and chief of those who did turn out confined their attention to the ancient Third . . ."[14]

The reference is to the Third Ward or French part of the city.

But by 1857 the value of the tourist trade became evident to Americans, who formed the Mystik Crewe of Comus, the first of the present Mardi Gras organizations, to revive the idea of parading the streets. This changed the French tradition into an American celebration, so that in 1859 the *Daily Delta* was able to say:

"Mardi Gras"

"The last day of Carnival went off with more than usual spirit on the part of the inhabitants and the old custom of maskers parading the streets was somewhat revived yesterday."[15]

During the 19th century these Mardi Gras parades employed New Orleans musicians. As the parades grew to huge dimensions in modern times the small New Orleans bands were eliminated in favor of the big professional parade bands imported for the occasion from around the country.

There are other parades, seldom seen by visitors to the Mardi Gras and even unknown to some residents. In the suburbs of the city there are a number of smaller Carnival clubs which hold parades on Mardi Gras day. Composed of white-middle class people, these clubs still employ the New Orleans traditional colored bands for their parades. They are arduous jobs for the musicians, beginning at 6 a.m. and lasting all day, covering several miles of suburban streets. For this employment the bands play popular songs and hit parade numbers, tunes familiar to the participants and spectators. A different repertoire is required for the different social environment. New Orleans musicians play all kinds of music as their business cards always state, *Music for all Occasions*, but the style remains unique and each type of music is equally pleasing and "inspiriting."

The day after Mardi Gras is Ash Wednesday the start of the Lenten season when from the musician's standpoint the town, so to speak, is temporarily closed down. In the Catholic tradition of the city music is thought by much of the population to be incompatible with Lent.

An illustration of this attitude occurred in the 1920s when a club in the suburb of Algiers hired the Henry Allen (Snr.) Brass Band to play for their Carnival parade. The chosen assembly place for the band was a large corner barroom close to the Algiers police station. Here the band gathered before dawn at 5 a.m. on a cold winter morning. Upon arrival the first order of business was the need to obtain outer and inner warmth.

When the men entered the bar they were surprised to find an all-night Mardi Gras party in progress. The musicians were gleefully welcomed, provided with drinks and asked to play a tune so the celebrants could dance. The Allen band, noted for its musical excellence but not for its abstinence, readily agreed. At the conclusion of the tune the band was heartily applauded more drinks were supplied and an encore requested. In this way the time passed swiftly and enjoyably.

Later, when someone drew the shades from the windows it was seen to be daylight, time for the band to join the Mardi Gras parade. Unsteadily the musicians made their way out of the bar, lining up in a ragged formation. At full volume they blasted into a popular tune and began to stagger along the street. Immediately doors and windows flew open as astonished people looked to see what was happening. And from the police station a stampede of indignant policemen came charging down the street waving their batons and shouting for the band to stop. Abruptly the bemused musicians were hustled off to the station house wondering what the fuss was all about.

It seems the band had enjoyed the hospitality of the barroom longer than intended; twenty-four hours longer, to be precise. Not only had they missed the parade of Shrove Tuesday, they had been arrested for disturbing the Lenten peace of Ash Wednesday.[16]

The local brass bands of New Orleans were able to retain the ancient music traditions of the city considerably longer than the dance bands because they continued to receive support from the neighborhood societies and were not subjected to exploitive commercial pressures. That was particularly true of the Eureka Brass Band, successor of the Excelsior, New Orleans' most famous brass band. Although the Eureka was a relatively small ten-piece band it retained a valid echo of earlier bands. The elderly musicians, born and raised in the 19th century, took pride in continuing to play music in the same manner as the great Creole bands, even to using a part of the repertoire. As a result, until the late 1950s it was still possible to hear traditional Creole brass band music on the streets of the city.

Professional recording was then difficult to arrange because of segregation and a lack of interest by recording companies. At almost the last minute a fortunate 1958 recording by the historian Sam Charters captured for posterity the sound of the Eureka Brass Band.

New Orleans street parade snapshots

Members of the George Williams Brass Band. Left to right are Edward Washington, Steve Poree and George Williams.

Leader of the Young Tuxedo Brass Band John Casimir fastens a music card to his E flat clarinet. Over his right shoulder can be seen the cymbal attached to the bass drum.

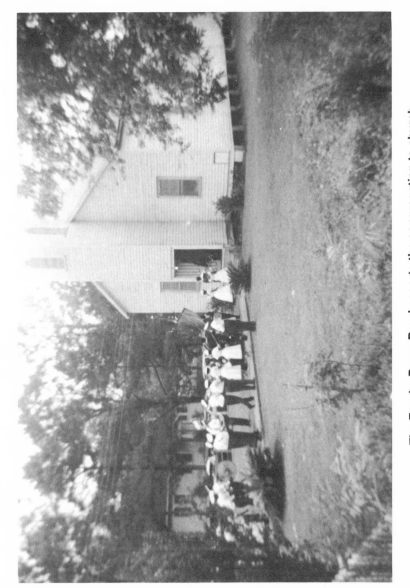

The Eureka Brass Band escorts the congregation to church.

Three "Kids" play a parade. Left to right are Kid Sheik, Kid Clayton and Kid Thomas.

Avery "Kid" Howard and Mrs. Howard.

CHAPTER 12

THE RECONSTRUCTION PERIOD

Before the Civil War, under the yoke of the slave system, Creole society was silenced by the black code laws. After Union troops were withdrawn from the South, Creoles again were suppressed although not so completely, by the Jim Crow laws of segregation. In the interim years of the Reconstruction period, under Federal Government protection, the Creoles became deeply involved in the attempt to bring democracy to Louisiana. It can be viewed as the desperate struggle of a highly cultured minority group battling against a majority led by the wealthy planters determined to reimpose conditions similar to slavery. A contest doomed to failure for the Creoles when the support of the Union Army was removed in 1877.

An important part of the Creole effort was the publication of newspapers which were almost totally occupied with the political events of that turbulent age. Sometimes there were social affairs reported or a small social column in which it is possible to catch a glimpse of Creole community affairs. This period is our last opportunity to observe the Creoles as a separate society. Increasingly after Emancipation they became involved with the goals of the freed slaves until the two groups are no longer distinguishable in the print media.

In this chapter we will observe some of the social events of the Creoles and the colored people of New Orleans during the Reconstruction and post-Reconstruction era. Documenting for the first time how the music of New Orleans developed during that period and revealing the social environment which enabled it to do so.

Even before the Civil War more than a hundred Creoles raised a capital of $30,000 to finance the publication of a French language newspaper named *L'Union* intended to serve the Creole community. A courageous enterprise in view of the stringent laws against all non-white owned publications. Laws carrying penalties of life imprisonment or death at the discretion of the court. Moreover it is apparent that the men deliberately and defiantly challenged those laws by openly publishing their names in the paper.

The first printing of *L'Union* was issued on February 1, 1857. Monsieur A. Malespine was named as managing director with Messieurs E. Dumez and E. Lamuloniere as the first editors. Later Paul Trevigne and Nelson Fouche were added to the editorial staff. This newspaper along with other Creole publications has been largely ignored by conventional historians of New Orleans. It is of importance for those serious scholars who wish to understand something of the Creole society before and during the Civil War.

As *L'Union* was chiefly concerned with the momentous happenings of the times there is little in the paper about such mundane activities as music. But on July 21, 1864, two years after the Federal occupation of the city, *L'Union* was replaced by the *New Orleans Tribune*, or *La Tribune de la Nouvelle Orleans*. It was founded by Dr. Louis Roudanez and was printed in French and English. The editors were Paul Trevigne and a M. Dallaz who, we are told, was not a Creole but was from Belgium. The publishing of this bi-lingual newspaper signified an important change in the attitude of the Creole population relating to their place in the general community. *L'Union* had been published by and for the French speaking Creoles. A well educated minority population within the slave system but a class apart, not slave and not totally free. With the change to the *Tribune*, Creoles made known their decision to unite their cause with that of the slaves, then on the brink of emancipation. To become the educated leaders of the illiterate mass of freed Black people. Indeed on August 11, 1864 the paper referred to the slaves as "our dormant partners." Intended as the standard bearer for all anti-Confederate, anti-slavery factions, the *Tribune* took an even bolder political stance than its predecessor. In its first editorial the paper stated:

"Under the above title we publish a new paper devoted to the principles heretofore defended by the *Union*. Convinced that

L'UNION

Jeudi, 18 Juin 1857 — NOUVELLE-ORLÉANS N°8 & 80, RUE ROYALE. Vol. 1. — No. 13.

ABONNEMENT A L'UNION

JOURNAL QUOTIDIEN DU MATIN

TARIF DES ANNONCES

A. MALESPINE, Gérant.

1857 Masthead of the Creole newspaper L'Union. The only non-white newspaper in the slave South.

a newspaper, under the present circumstances, representing the principles and interests which we propose to defend and advocate was much needed in New Orleans, we shall spare no means at our command to render the *Tribune* worthy of public confidence and respect and these were the reasons which prompted us to its publication.

Satisfied that we shall meet with encouragement from every friend of progress and civilization, we have purchased the interest and material of the *Union*—a paper which we acknowledge to have well-fitted its mission however humble may have been this organ of an oppressed class during the past three years of our social change and reform . . .

The publishers of this paper can fully appreciate the great responsibility under which they have placed themselves, but being satisfied that this is the time for every citizen to do the most he can for the Union, freedom and true republican progress, they have undertaken the severe task hoping to meet with the strong support of every friend of progress and liberty."

To emphasize its position the front page of the first issue contained an article condemning the black code laws. In part it said:

". . . The black code of Louisiana is as bloody and as barbarous as the laws against witchcraft . . . It has been practically repealed by the authority of public sentiment ever since the occupation of Louisiana by the national forces. When we say public sentiment we of course do not allude to the prejudices of rebels, but to the enlightened opinions of loyal citizens, the only members of the community whose sentiments on public matters have, or should have any weight."

This article then went on to describe in detail some of the "bloody and barbarous" Black code laws, leaving no doubt the Creoles were intent upon abolishing the laws of the slave State and completely reforming Louisiana.

To some extent this position had been forced upon them. In 1863 they applied for the Right to register and vote—Rights they were supposed to have acquired by the treaty of 1803. They were told by General Banks, then in charge of the Union Army at New Orleans that they would not receive those Rights. No distinction was to be made between the freed slaves and the Creoles of color. Not until the passage of the Thirteenth, Fourteenth and Fifteenth Amendments to the Constitution did the Creoles attain full citizenship in the same manner as the ex-slaves. An ironic situation considering the Creoles were among the best educated, most qualified people in Louisiana perhaps in the entire South, to become citizens of the United States. Moreover, they had earned that Right. Three regiments of the Free Colored People of New Orleans had served with the Union Army under General Butler and had distinguished themselves by their bravery on the battlefield. We are told:

"... The free colored men of New Orleans flew to arms. One of the regiments of a thousand men was completed in fourteen days. In a very few weeks, General Butler had his three regiments of infantry and two batteries of artillery enrolled, equipped, officered, drilled and ready for service. Better soldiers never shouldered arms. They were zealous, attentive, obedient and intelligent. No men in the Union Army had such a stake in the contest as they. Few understood it as well as they..."[17]

These units later became the Seventy-Fourth, Seventy-Fifth and Seventy-Sixth regiments of the United States Army.

Another report tell us:

"The first and second Louisiana and the 'Native Guard' regiment of free Negroes ... were billeted in the Judah Touro building and every afternoon they paraded with zest to the music of their band."[18]

General Butler certainly deserves credit for inducting the Free Colored volunteer soldiers into the Union Army on September 27, 1862, but the Creoles had organized themselves militarily long before New Orleans was occupied by the Federal forces. In 1861 a newspaper reported:

"The Native Guards are of the opinion, just as companies of white men, they can as well have a lively time until the enemy invade our soil. One of these companies of colored regiments named, we believe, the Beauregard Guards, was presented on Saturday night with a fine silk flag by a young lady of the second district and another company of the same regiment, commanded by Captain Louis Lalane turned out yesterday with a brass band. In both cases a pleasant collation followed the military manifestation."[19]

Inevitably the Creole soldiers suffered casualties in the course of the Civil War. At the battle of Port Hudson Captain Andre Caillioux of the Native Guards was mortally wounded. When his body was returned to New Orleans he was honored with a hero's funeral on July 11, 1863. More than thirty-five lodges, societies and associations were present in the funeral procession, which was said to be over a mile long. These organizations represented the Fraternal, Civic, Masonic, Benevolent and Religious groups of the Creole people of New Orleans. (Listed in the Appendix)

With the return of the Confederate soldiers at the close of the Civil War there were complaints of renewed harassment. The *Tribune* reported a "colored funeral" in the uptown district was attacked by "white rowdies" of whom the paper said:

"Men who have served the rebellion for four years, men who have fought for the perpetuity of slavery come back to this city and though their hands are still stained with the blood of Union soldiers, they reign over us and gradually take control of civic and judicial affairs." (March 22, 1865.)

Southern whites had been defeated in war but their racially prejudiced attitude had not undergone any change. They had no intention of allowing Blacks to have the rights of free men. Before Congress enacted the Reconstruction programs the southern States passed laws with the intent of reimposing the Black codes. Black people were forbidden arms. Trespassing and vagrancy laws were so worded that anyone could be arrested at any time and hired out at hard labor. There were "apprenticeship" laws to force children to work, and Blacks could not change their jobs. In a hypocritical attempt to conceal their true intention these post-Civil War laws often made no mention of race. They were repealed by the Reconstruction governments but many were re-enacted later under the Jim Crow segregation system.

About this time the wealthy landowners and planters began their propaganda to present slavery as a system that had been kind and gentle to the slaves. The *Tribune* did not fail to respond. From time to time it carried reports of slave treatment:

141

"The way planters and overseers showed kindness to female slaves is well illustrated by the following instance which took place on the plantation of Mr. Tom Duval at Springfield parish of East Baton Rouge. It was in July and the heat was very oppressive. At the time of going to work a black woman complained of being sick but she was told she had to work anyhow. She went to the cornfield but soon returned, seriously ill.

The lash was applied to her.

She then went back again, but was not seen in the evening. A few days later her corpse was found in the cornfield. She had died of pain and exposure . . .

We could bring forth many other cases of a similar character. It shows the tender care planters took of their female slaves." (September 4, 1866.)

Reading sickening reports of this nature in the *Tribune*, the devastating effects of slavery on the southern white population is apparent. Effects from which the South and perhaps the entire nation has not yet fully recovered. The treatment of the slaves was appalling but the cost to the whites was the loss of their humanity. While pretending to the belief that Black people were sub-human it was the white people who actually became sub-human in their outlook and in their behavior. The tragic result of the corrupting influence of power over others. Creole editors and writers of the *Tribune* shattered the long conspiracy of silence which had concealed the evils of slavery. In so doing they showed they had lost none of the courage their forebears had demonstrated when they rebelled against Spanish rule in the previous century, the first such rebellion opposing colonialism on the American continent.

Although the Civil War freed the slaves it did not destroy the plantation system which had been the impelling motive for American slavery. Planters were still powerful, with a great deal of influence. They struck back at the *Tribune* through the State legislature. The New Orleans *Daily Crescent* of December 16, 1865 reported a bill had been introduced to the Louisiana Senate by a Mr. Munday "to punish persons inciting to insurrection or revolt in the State." A Mr. Mohan suggested an amendment reading "inciting to insurrection or revolt by publication, addresses or otherwise." He said "there was, as everybody knew, an insurrectionary sheet published in this city called the *Tribune* which had been inciting certain classes of population by warning and innuendoes about the massacres in San Domingo and Jamaica and threatening the same calamities here. The Press is free was an acknowledged axiom; but that freedom must be curtailed when it encroaches to such an extent.":

The Creole staff of the *Tribune* must have felt a sense of resolute satisfaction in the knowledge their "insurrectionary sheet" was a cause of discomfiture to those who had for so long oppressed them.

In the meantime the Creoles continued to maintain, as well as they could, their small oasis of culture within the great southern desert of the *beaux arts*. Some of the musicians cited by Desdunes were giving performances at the Orleans Theater. On August 22, 1865 the *Tribune* announced:

"This evening the Orleans Theater will be once more a place of attraction for our population. A great performance will be given for the benefit of our distinguished artist Mr. S. Snaer. The programme contains a happy choice of musical pieces and merry 'Vaudevilles'. On the musical compositions of Mr. S. which will be executed this evening we will not expatiate...but we must mention the fact that the great symphony composed by Edmond Dede, our well known fellow citizen, which was so enthusiastically received on the French stage, will be among the pieces to be executed.

Our favorite artists and 'amateurs'...will be there, Mr. Eugene McCarty, Mr. C. V. Florette and the whole chorus of young ladies. The performance at the Orleans Theater have not to be considered as a means of amusement only; we should feel proud of the talent exhibited there by our friends and we should contribute to the promotion and progress of our distinguished brothers and sisters."

The next day the *Tribune*, now calling itself "The Official Organ of the Universal Suffrage Party" reported:

"Mr. Samuel Snaer's concer and theatrical performance was a great success; everybody acted his part with great ability and no one regretted the time passed at the Orleans Theater last evening."

143

A few weeks later the *Tribune* again remarked upon Mr. Snaer's activities:

"We have just received a copy of the song 'Rapelle Toi' by Mr. A. Mussett, music by Mr. S. Snaer, the talented Louisianian." (October 10, 1865.)

Under the various Reconstruction governments of Louisiana, southern reactionary prejudice was never far beneath the surface of social affairs. Creoles had always been allowed to attend the French Opera House using the second tier for segregated seating. As an indication of the way Creoles had become equated with the ex-slaves, an attempt was made to prohibit their presence at the Opera which the *Tribune* was quick to report:

"Another Outrage"

"Mr. E. V. McCarty, a respectable gentleman of polished manner was [kept] out of the Opera House on Tuesday evening because he is a colored man. There was perhaps not a man in the whole audience who was more fit than Mr. McCarty . . . Let the members of the legislature set down this outrage upon their note book and the moment comes to vote for the civil rights bill, do their duty by passing that instrument." (January 21, 1869.)

After performing valiantly on behalf of the Creoles and the freed slaves for several years, the *Tribune* suspended publication in 1870. It was immediately succeeded by the *Louisianian*, a newspaper largely devoted to the chaotic politics of the Reconstruction era in Louisiana. The editor was Mr. William G. Brown, from 1872 to 1876 the superintendent of schools in Louisiana, but the paper was under the direction of Senator, later Lt. Governor, P. B. S. Pinchback a colored politician who had migrated to Louisiana.[20] The reporters, probably friends of Pinchback brought from the North, were impressed by the entertainments provided by the Creoles and the New Orleans citizenry. Fortunately for our purposes they thought the various community activities, particularly those attended by Pinchback and other colored politicians, were deserving of notice in print.

Eventually the paper developed a small social column in which the names of bands and musicians occasionally appeared. By sampling a representative number of these comments on New Orleans social affairs we can discern in some degree the development of the city's musical life during the post-Civil War years.

On February 16, 1871 the *Louisianian* reported:

"Francs-Amis"

"Availing ourself of our complimentary we repaired to the Hall of the Francs Amis on Saturday evening last, and participated in the hilarities and enjoyments we found in full blast on our arrival. The lovers of the dance kept up a constant tripping of 'the light fantastic toe', till the supper hour arrived when the company in groups and little congenial knots gathered round the tempting repast and earnestly discussed the qualities of the viands and the wines. The ladies were finely bedecked and presented an array of natural and artificial beauty perfectly admirable... We noticed among the most prominent, Senators Pinchback, Ingraham, Hunsacker; Representatives Morphy, Kenner, F. C. Antoine, Raby. The indefatigable exertions of Capt. W. H. Green, Mr. St. Cyr and other managers contributed greatly to the ease and enjoyment of all present and we enjoyed 'a nice time'."

This description of a Creole dance would have been equally suitable applied to similar social affairs in the mid-20th century, even to the usual New Orleans appreciative comment of "a nice time."

The reporter so enjoyed the dance at the Francs Amis Hall that he decided to repeat the experience at the Economy Hall. Here he reveals he is not a Creole for he confesses his inability to dance, something Creoles were taught from childhood.[21] This is regrettable as he is unable to make any observations of the dances or the music for them, still he did not fail to notice the legendary beauty of the Creole women:

"Economy Hall"

"A few evenings since we had the pleasure of attending by

complimentary from those genial whole-souled gentlemen Messrs. Caplin and Relf, a very select character Ball at Economy Hall. Many of the ladies represented various historical and traditional characters. But our belief is the young lady who personated the Indian girl did it to perfection. We will not be so invidious as to call names, but we must say that there were several ladies present whose youth, winning smiles, graces and beauty entitle them to special notice.

We don't dance; but we love 'music and dancing and chatting with the Belles', and so we enjoyed our visit to the Economy and cherish pleasant recollections." (February 26, 1871.)

After the Civil War many of the freed slaves left the plantations surrounding New Orleans, moving to the city in large numbers to seek an education and wage-paying work. The majority had settled in the expanding uptown district where several meeting halls had been built for their educational and recreational use. Two prominent uptown halls of this post-Civil War period were the Mechanics Institute and the National Hall, both of which were visited by the *Louisianian* reporter:

"Last night closed the week's entertainment at the National Hall. The premiums won the five nights previous were awarded ... We love rational enjoyment and approve any effort to improve the general tone and therefore we approve the efforts of our friend C. F. Ladd ... The Hall has been tastefully fitted up and the ladies have been indefatigable in their exertions ... We understand the prime object of the entertainment to be to obtain funds in aid of the First Baptist New Church on Common Street and we believe there will be tolerably good 'net proceeds' to be turned over." (March 2, 1871.)

On Friday May 13, 1871, there were three picnics in City Park where, we are informed, "Kelly's Band" was in attendance. This was Thomas Kelly, a colored musician whose brass band was becoming popular. Little is known of him other than he was a highly skilled Creole musician who performed in concert on the same stage with Creole luminaries such as Samuel Snaer.

A month later there was a notice in the *Louisianian* concerning the Creole Brass Band:

146

"Arrival of General Warner
A Serenade and a Speech"

"General Warner the recently appointed collector of customs at the port arrived in the city on Wednesday morning.

On the evening of the same day quite a crowd of prominent colored Republicans accompanied by the Creole brass band called on him to pay their respects . . . " (July 20, 1871)

Although this is a rare mention in print, the Creole Brass Band undoubtedly had been in existence for many years and may have been just one of several bands composed of Creole musicians using the generic title. It is entirely possible this was the same band that played for the Portuguese parade which had received newspaper notice some fifteen years earlier.

The ancient Creole custom of the serenade was a very common occurrence throughout the history of New Orleans. As in other aspects of New Orleans music, the serenade has a strictly European tradition reaching back to medieval times. Sadly the practice seems to have ended, along with many another of the city's musical customs, during the depression of the 1930s.

Almost any event could serve as an excuse for a serenade. For example, Mrs. Charlotte McCullum Boutinet, in conversation with the author, recalled her delight when as a child she was accorded a serenade by her father's band—the George McCullum Snr. Band—on the occasion of her birthday. Creole musicians were especially fond of serenades because it brought so much pleasure to the recipients and because the music was always played "soft and sweet". Which brings to mind Jelly Roll Morton's admonition to the effect that New Orleans music is to be played soft and sweet with plenty of rhythm.

The staff of Northerners of the *Louisianian* were pleasantly surprised and flattered by the custom of the Creole serenade. They thought it deserving of record in print when they were provided with the courtesy:

"Serenade"
"The compliment paid the Editor and Manager of the Louisianian by that band of serenaders on Friday night is

147

hereby acknowledged. They discoursed sweet music to us." (July 23, 1871)

At this period of the development of New Orleans music it was not unusual for both a string band and a brass band to appear at a social event. On August 13, 1871, the *Louisianian* carried this advertisement notice:

> "Grand Vocal and Instrumental Concert
> at the Mechanics Institute
> Tuesday August 15, 1871"

"Kelly's celebrated silver cornet band will be in attendance to enliven the occasion. An excellent string band under the leadership of Mr. Frank Dodson will, after the close of the concert, amuse all lovers of dancing..."

In its report of this event the *Louisianian* said:

"... The entertainment lasted till 11 p.m. when the concert being over the center of the spacious hall was cleared, a band of music made its appearance and the lovers of the dance went in with their accustomed relish and kept up the enjoyment till a late hour."

It should be noted in 1871 the brass band played for the concert but the traditional string band still played for the dance.

Another indication of the popularity of dancing was this *Louisianian* report:

"Last Saturday evening The United Sons of America had a monster entertainment at the National Hall in this city. At an early hour the hall was well filled and the cry was 'still they come'. Dancing was the order of the evening and it was kept up with little intermission all through the night. A well prepared supper table, cakes, fruits and all the etceteras which complete a fine lay out were there..." (September 28, 1871)

In the midst of this gaiety the newspaper constantly warned its readers of the incipient reaction to the Reconstruction programs of the United States evinced by the former slaveholders and the ex-Confederates. The Ku Klux Klan, the White League, the Knights of the White Camillia and other terrorist groups were making their presence known throughout the southern

States by lynching, torture and murder. Perhaps with the hope of intimidating the white reactionaries of New Orleans, on October 5, 1871 there was a parade reported of the "Stanton Guards" which was preceded by the Columbia Band and Drum Corps under the direction of William Carter.

A few days later, on October 10, Kelly's Brass Band again appeared at the Mechanic's Institute. On this occasion Mr. A. P. Williams, at the piano, accompanied a choir of young ladies. And on October 19 the *Louisianian* informed its readers of another social event:

"Concert Tonight"

"This evening there will be a first rate entertainment at the Lyceum Hall . . . Messrs. A. P. Williams, H. A. Corbin, Thos. Kelly, Alfred White and Professor Snaer will perform . . ."

There was a police parade reported on December 21. These were the New Orleans Metropolitans, a small, mostly colored police force charged with keeping the peace in the city during the Reconstruction years. The paper said: ". . . Two bands of music were in attendance and by the performance of inspiring and appropriate airs merited approbation."

The "Young Female Benevolent Society" held a "Grand Concert and Exhibition" at Lyceum Hall on March 13, 1872, at which we are informed the string band of Mr. Samuel Davis provided the music.[22]

The *Louisianian* for April 18, 1872, gave an account of a serenade by a brass band:

"Serenade"

"On Friday night last, a number of gentlemen accompanied by Kelly's brass band gave a fine serenade to Hon. Frederick Douglas at the residence of Lieut. Governor Pinchback.

Mr. Douglas and Governor Pinchback both appeared, and the former addressed a few appropriate remarks to the party, at the conclusion of which, three rousing cheers were given for Douglas and calls for Pinchback; the Lieutenant Governor informed them that, instead of responding to them in speech, he would invite them inside to refresh the inner man, which was cordially accepted and the party, after regaling themselves, left playing a lively air."

A month later the newspaper reported another serenade for Pinchback, this time by a Mississippi River Steamboat band:

"On Monday night last the band of the steamer 'Mary Houston' gave a fine serenade to Lieutenant Governor Pinchback which was duly acknowledged." (May 18, 1872)

It can be seen from this notice there were bands, probably Creole string bands, playing on the Riverboats in 1872, half a century earlier than conventional histories have supposed New Orleans music was spread by this means.

House parties at times were reported by the paper. On May 4, 1872, it advised its readers that General A. E. Barber had given a house party with "a fine string band of music."

Nor were picnics neglected by the *Louisianian* reporters:

"Picnics have been all the rage during the week. Every day has found large numbers hurrying out of the heart of the city to find recreation and amusement in the various resorts. [At one picnic] A fine band of music sent out delightful strains, and in the cool of the day lively airs attracted many a dancer to the stand." (May 25, 1872)

Sometimes these picnics were marathon affairs. The members of the Pelican Lodge gave notice that after parading through the city they would have a picnic at City Park. In reporting this event the newspaper observed:

"The Pelican Lodge K. C. and their numerous friends had a gay old time at the City Park with their picnic which lasted for three days . . ." (June 15, 1872)

The ancient custom of the serenade had been performed by string bands in Europe and in New Orleans until the mid-19th century when, as we have seen, brass bands were also used for serenades in the city. The tradition of the string band serenade, however, still continued:

"Lieutenant Governor Pinchback returns his thanks to the serenaders who visited him with that fine string band on Monday night . . ." (July 6, 1872)

A house party at Pinchback's residence enables us to learn of an additional Creole musician. The paper remarked on November 2, 1872, that at this social affair the people were "busily engaged in 'tripping the light fantastic toe' to the tune and time of one of Charles Jaeger's inspiring pieces..."

Jaeger's name again appears in the newspaper in connection with a picnic:

"The first picnic of the season was given by the teachers and scholars of St. Andrew's School... as we neared the scene of amusement our ears were pleasantly greeted by the sounds of sweet music from Jaeger's splendid band..." (May 9, 1874)

A few days later a break or "crevasse" appeared in the levee of the Mississippi river several miles upriver from New Orleans. Even this event seemingly required music:

"Persons desirous of visiting the Bonnet Carre crevasse have the opportunity offered them tomorrow (Sunday) 17th, on board the splendid steamer Empire, leaving the wharf at 12 o'clock M. returning at 8 p.m. A brass band will be on board for the occasion..." (May 16, 1874)

On May 30, another school picnic was reported and here again we see the two types of bands, brass and string, present at one social affair:

"Sumner Boy's School Picnic"

"One of the most enjoyable picnics of the season was given on Thursday last at the City Park by the above named school. The arrangements were complete and reflect much credit upon Professor Williams and the ladies in charge. The music by Kelly's Brass Band and also by the string band under the leadership of Professor Richardson was excellent and afforded full opportunity for the enjoyment thereof..."

On September 17, 1874, there occurred what is known to history as the White League Riot of New Orleans, in which, it was reported, two thousand white rioters "ambushed" three hundred Metropolitan policemen. This disorder was suppressed with the aid of Federal troops. The *Louisianian* published an extra edition on October 3, which contained an article concerning the "reign of terror", appealing for harmony between the races. It said in part:

"No state can boast of more wealthy, intelligent and refined colored men than Louisiana, and yet it is hardly possible to conceive of less official respect and consideration to character and ability than it is our misfortune to receive from the powers that be . . ."

The article was signed by fourteen members of "the executive committee" including two musicians—E. V. McCarty and H. A. Corbin.

A Louisiana Creole from Shreveport, Mr. C. C. Antoine, had replaced Pinchback as Lieutenant Governor. He was duly serenaded by the "Bell-Decker Band." The *Louisianian* wrote of strains of music enlivening the neighborhood: "invited to enter . . . the band discoursed some of their sweetest airs . . ." (October 24, 1874)

This first mention of the Bell-Decker Band has some significance. Here we are witness to the birth of the most famous of all New Orleans brass bands. This band became known as Decker's Band under the leadership of Sylvester Decker until 1879, it was then named the Excelsior Band and continued under that name until the depression of the 1930s contributing six decades of musical service to the New Orleans social community. Many of the most respected Creole musicians were members of this band. For example, cornetist Edward (Edwarre) Clem who occasionally substituted for Bolden and played in the Eagle Band that was formed from the Bolden Band; Honore Dutrey the trombonist in Joe Oliver's Creole Jazz Band, and George Baquet, regarded by his contemporaries as the greatest of all New Orleans clarinet players.[23]

After attending a Creole ball at the Economy Hall the *Louisianian* social reporter became almost rhapsodic in his brief account and we see that he had learned to recognize two of the most popular dances:

"The Grand Fancy Dress and Calico Ball given by the Young Veterans for the benefit of their relief fund last night—St.

Joseph's—at the Economy Hall was a brilliant affair. Delightful music, fair forms and lovely faces with the consonance of gentle hearts palpitating against manly bosoms in Waltz and Mazurka added to the charm of the evening." (March 20, 1875)

The New Orleans French Opera House had been under pressure from the white reactionaries to deny attendance to the Creole people. Not surprisingly this had resulted in a severe loss of funds. With few exceptions white patrons of the lively arts or any form of higher cultural pursuit were conspicuous by their absence in the South. In an article headed "French Opera at the Economy Hall" the *Louisianian* for May 15, 1875 said:

"During the past winter Manager Canonge of the Opera House, yielding the clamor of the white league and its foolish prejudices, denied to our educated and refined colored ladies and gentlemen desirous of visiting that place of amusement, equal accommodation with other portions of the public.

The previous winter, when the Opera House was open to all respectable patrons and no such invidious distinctions occurred, manager Canonge reaped a harvest from the result of his efforts for the public, adequately compensating him for the large outlay incurred. The past winter, the affectations of caste prejudices by certain patrons caused him to adopt a course, which, closing the doors of the Opera to a wealthy and appreciative class, also lost him the sum of many thousands of dollars, otherwise received, and obliged the closing of the Opera House with a failure to pay the singers. These, appealing to the public, were tendered a benefit by the owners and managers of the Societe Economic, M. Aristide Mary, and other gentlemen . . ."

The Colored Creoles, it was reported, had raised sufficient funds to pay for the opera company's return to France.

The central part of the city was by no means exclusively the site of parades; the suburbs also had their festivities:

"Our Carrolton colored fire companies had a delightful celebration on their annual parade last Saturday . . . they paraded through the principle streets of our suburban city with banners flying, flags waving and under the inspiration of music which fairly infected the town; causing the infusion of good cheer to everybody within sight and hearing, and giving a pleasure long to be remembered by all present . . ." (June 5, 1875)

Excursions by boat up and down the river were a common occurrence; with the arrival of the railroad that activity was soon extended to the train:

"The Grand Excursion to Bay St. Louis under the auspices of the United States Relief Association takes place Monday the 19th inst. A special train has been engaged and Professor Martin's Brass Band, so well and favorably known for its musical excellence, will be in attendance . . ." (July 17, 1875)

In a brief notice of a "presentation" at the residence of Mr. O. J. Dunn, on September 4 1875 the paper said Decker's Brass Band was in attendance. Sylvester Decker evidently had assumed the sole leadership of this band.

Funerals were not wholly overlooked by the *Louisianian*. Reporting the funeral for General Barber of the State Militia the paper wrote of the procession "preceded by Kelly's Band playing slow music." (October 30, 1875)

A description of a concert mentioned a Professor Denis, probably intended to refer to Professor Davis:

"The Grand Concert of our friends of the Economy Aid Association . . . was a highly agreeable affair, Professor Denis, so well and favorably known for his musical ability presided at the piano . . ." (December 25, 1875)

A larger concert, this one probably involving musicians of the Creole Philharmonic Orchestra, was also reported:

"The concert given at Globe Hall last Monday night was a decided success. The solos, duets and trios were skillfully executed. The most notable features of the entertainment was the orchestra composed of about twenty colored men, whose renditions of several difficult overtures, symphonies etc. evidenced careful training and reflected credit upon their accomplished leader, Professor Louis Martin. New Orleans is probably the only city in the United States that can boast of an orchestra, complete in all its details, composed entirely of colored men.

The concert was of itself, more than equivalent for the price of admission, but in order to make the measure full, the entertainment closed with dancing which was kept up to a late hour and afforded pleasure to all who participated." (October 20, 1877)

It should be noted Professor Martin not only led a brass band which played music suitable for excursionists, he was also the leader of this large Philharmonic Orchestra. Furthermore, that orchestra not only played classical music concerts, it also played music for dancing. Evidence once again that Creole musicians drew no distinction between the various types and styles of music. It was all considered to be simply music based on the same principles.

For much of the year 1878 there was a widespread epidemic of Yellow Fever; the *Louisianian* suspended publication for several months and with the approach of the Mardi Gras of 1879 wrote:

"A Mardi Gras observation—let us eat drink and be merry today for tomorrow Yellow Jack may rule the roost." (February 15, 1879)

The citizens seem to have agreed with this philosophy which promoted the paper to write:

"After the storm, the calm, is an old but true maxim. Amusements of all kinds have been going the rounds for the last two or three weeks, keeping up a continual strain on one, both physically and financially. There is a scarcity of them now and the young, gay and 'flashy' have moments of quiet in which to recuperate and get 'fixed' sufficient to meet the tidal wave of mirth and pleasure, which will commence its sweeping, surging motion on the 7th and last with little interruption for the next six or eight weeks." (June 7, 1879)

On May 31, 1879 the Pride of Jefferson Lodge announced an excursion to Thibodeaux with "Decker's Band in full uniform." Reporting later on this affair the newspaper said upon their arrival: "As soon as possible a procession was formed with Decker's band leading and carrying the unsophisticated into ecstasies at the music so grand and sweet." (June 14, 1879)

This reference to "the unsophisticated" presumably refers

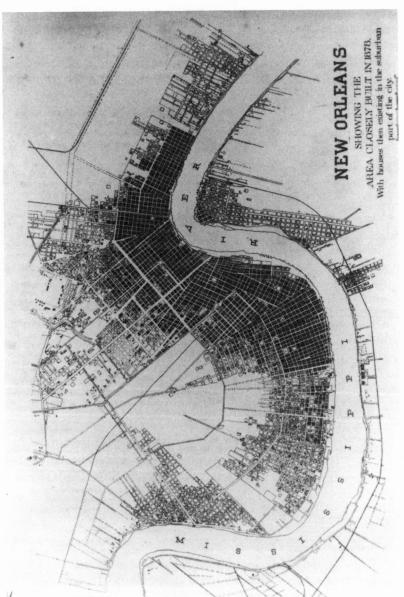

Map of the "Crescent City" in 1878.

to Thibodeaux residents who were unfamiliar with the music of New Orleans. It could have been applied equally well to all the South; indeed, all the world beyond the New Orleans environs at that time was unaware of New Orleans music.

Another excursion, this one by steamboat to Baton Rouge, was announced on June 21. The notice said the trip would take place July 3rd, when "A full Brass Band will accompany the excursion." In a later report of the event we learn this was the Excelsior Brass Band which only one month earlier was still called Decker's band. This must have been one of their first engagements under their new name. The paper notified its readers that after the excursionists disembarked at Baton Rouge:

". . . A line of procession was then formed and the commandery, as the guests of the Masons of Baton Rouge, paraded the principle streets with the Excelsior band uniformed at its head." (July 12, 1879)

It is clear from this report that although Baton Rouge was the second largest city in Louisiana, it did not have any brass bands. With only a few exceptions in later years, the musicians of New Orleans supplied the music for all of Louisiana and the South.

The open space at the rear of Orleans street was originally used as a recreation area by the slave population of New Orleans, because of this the racists of the slave society named it Congo Plains. Later, as the town grew around the place, it became Congo Park. Finally, as the area shrank still further, it was called Congo Square. Always as a nickname, the name was never officially recognized by the city even in the darkest days of slavery. At first this nickname was not meant to refer to the type of dancing that was performed there. It is reasonably certain those who so named the place would not have recognized "Congo dancing" if such a thing has ever existed, nor distinguished it from other forms of dancing. The nickname was intended as a racist label for the park used by Black people, not as a description of their dancing. Tales of wild voodoo orgies, African rituals and Congo dances were fabricated at a much later period to encourage the 19th-century tourist trade and incidentally enrich inventive writers. Perhaps it is redundant to add these stories were always written by southern white authors.

In the pages of the *Louisianian* it can be seen the people who made use of the area had a more representative and logical name for the place. They called it Orleans Park:

"The complimentary picnic given by the 'Big Four' on last Tuesday the 19th inst. at Orleans Park was a happy affair. For courtesies extended we are indebted to Messrs. Barnet, Porter, Duplessis, Martinez and a score of young ladies who ably assisted the young men. The initial entertainment of the 'Big Four' was a success. Come again." (July 19, 1879)

The "Big Four" of Barnett, Porter, Duplessis and Martinez was a four-piece string band. Unfortunately we are not told anything of the instruments in the band. Presumably it was not very different from the string bands which played on the short and narrow balconies of the early dance halls—violins or violas, mandolin and guitar. At the time this eminently civilized picnic took place in Orleans Park or "Congo Square" in the heart of downtown New Orleans, Buddy Bolden was not yet two years old, living in the uptown part of the city.

Another picnic notice in the *Louisianian* informs us of another band:

"On last Monday the Jeunes Amis Benevolent Association gave their last picnic of the season. In the morning they paraded through the principle streets with Professor Wolf's Band and one hundred and seventy five members in rank . . . On the picnic grounds the goddess of pleasure reigned supreme. The beauty and respectability of our Creole population were out in large numbers. With excellent music, beautiful and graceful young ladies . . ." (September 20, 1879)

The same issue of the paper also tells us: "Mr. Leon Cuillette is the leader of the Excelsior Brass Band. He is a young musician of great promise."

For some unknown reason this first leader of the newly named band was soon replaced. A few weeks later the paper said: "Mr. Sylvester Decker has again assumed the leadership of the Excelsior Brass Band." (October 11, 1879)

About this time the *Louisianian* underwent a reorganization. Federal troops were withdrawn from the city in 1877, resulting in many supporters of the paper being ousted from their employment by the resurgent Democratic party dominated by southern racists. Consequently, financial assistance declined until the paper was able to publish only once a week. The new masthead read:

THE WEEKLY LOUISIANIAN
REPUBLICAN AT ALL TIMES AND
UNDER ALL CIRCUMSTANCES
THE ADVOCATE OF THE RIGHTS OF MAN

The post-Reconstruction city governments were careful not to discourage entertainments to distract the public as they consolidated their white supremacy policies. In the course of the next several years hundreds of social events requiring music were listed in the paper, a few mentioning the names of bands or musicians. Some further excerpts will be given in order to follow the continuing musical activity of the city. In this way it is hoped it will be possible to perceive something of the social environment in which the New Orleans musicians worked and further developed their music. Almost any type of community gathering was considered suitable for the presence of music including political assemblies:

"On last Monday evening, September 29th, the officers elect for the 3rd Ward Central Republican Club were formally installed. Their Hall on Peridido street was truly uncomfortably crowded, fully three hundred bona fide voters being present. Good order and decorem was preserved throughout . . . After adjournment, the club headed by the Pickwick Brass Band, paraded through several of the principal streets, partaking of a collation at the residence of Col. Antoine . . ." (October 4, 1879)

The Pickwick was an Algiers band formed in 1873 which had previously concentrated its efforts on engagements in the suburb of Algiers and the towns across the Mississippi River from New Orleans. It became one of the most popular bands of the city during the late 19th century. The band probably decided to expand its activities because there were so many opportunities to obtain work.[24] As the newspaper noted:

MCENERY AND PENN HAVING BEEN ELECTED GOVERNOR AND LIEUTENANT GOVERNOR BY THE WHITE PEOPLE, WERE DULY INSTALLED BY THIS OVERTHROW OF CARPETBAG GOVERNMENT OUST-ING THE USURPERS. GOV. KELLOGG.(WHITE) LIEUT. GOV. ANTOINE.(COLORED)

White supremacy inscriptions on a Canal Street obelisk.

UNITED STATES TROOPS TOOK OVER THE STATE
GOVERNMENT AND REINSTATED THE USURPERS
BUT THE NATIONAL ELECTION NOVEMBER 1876
RECOGNIZED WHITE SUPREMACY IN THE SOUTH
AND GAVE US OUR STATE.

These inscriptions on an obelisk erected on Canal street after the withdrawal of Union troops marked the end of the Reconstruction period in New Orleans.

"There seems to be no end to amusements. Balls, Soirees, Receptions and the like are crowding thick and fast upon us. This season promises, from present indications, to be the gayest of the gay. Tonight there will be a ball at the Exposition, Globe, Violet, Economy and Francs Amis halls, a dinner party on St. Andrews street and several private entertainments in the lower and upper portions of the city." (December 25, 1879)

And a few days later:

"The season so far has been an exceedingly gay one. Entertainment after entertainment has followed each other in quick succession and still they come." (January 3, 1880)

Our Creole historian, R. L. Desdunes, is frequently mentioned in the pages of the *Louisianian*, usually in connection with his work for the civil rights issue or for his efforts on behalf of the Masons:

"We are under obligation to Mr. R. L. Desdunes, chairman of the committee, for complimentary tickets to a grand anniversary ball to be given at the Masonic Hall . . . by the Louisiana Creole Lodge." (January 24, 1880)

A christening was considered an excellent occasion for music:

"Tuesday January 13th the residence of Mr. and Mrs. Alex J. Kenner presented a very brilliant appearance, a large and agreeable company of friends having gathered by formal invitation to witness the christening of Miss Helene Gertrude Kenner, the baby daughter of mine host and hostess . . . Around the festive board numerous toasts were drunk to the continued health and future prosperity of the babe . . . When the guests had adjourned to the parlour dancing was indulged in and kept up until nigh unto the morn . . ." (January 24, 1880)

In the social column of the newspaper we are fortunate to observe the beginning of the New Orleans Musicians Benevolent Society which ultimately became incorporated into the American Federation of Musicians as New Orleans Local 496:

"The ball given on Mardi Gras by the Excelsior Brass band

was a most decided financial success, clearing sufficient to purchase a new set of instruments from the well known warehouse of Louis Grunwald, esq. The success attending the effort of these young men has occasioned them to adopt a most excellent suggestion of one of their members; the formation of a Benevolent Association to be known as the Musicians Benevolent Society." (February 14, 1880)

On March 27, 1880 the *Louisianian* noted:
"There were seven Masquerade balls on St. Joseph's night among our people and all of them were well attended."
And on April 3rd:
"Six thousand persons attended the picnic of the Benevolent Sons of Louisiana at the Fair Grounds, Sunday."
Twelve hours of dancing, and therefore music playing, was not uncommon at a picnic:
"The Ladies of Progress Association will have a picnic July 5th at Loeper's Park, corner of Bienville and Alexander. Dancing from 11 a.m. to 11 p.m." (June 12, 1880)

To digress to another topic for a moment, on July 3, 1880 there was a story in the paper of a white man who had attempted to shoot a "negro" who had married his sister. The paper commented:
"If the brothers-in-law of the French kind were all to go a-gunning for the 'niggers' who have married their white sisters, we wonder how many of the male gender would be left above the sod."
This observation must have caused considerable laughter among the readers of the *Louisianian*. The social mores of the original French colonial city were founded on a philosophy of assimilation of all free races. The social policy of the later American city was exactly opposite; that is it was based upon segregation by race. But the earlier process of assimilation resulted in a situation where it has never been possible to know by skin color where the Black race ends and the White race begins in New Orleans.

References to the kind of dances then in vogue are rare, but

163

in reporting a dance held uptown at Cottrell's Hall the paper said:

". . . We noted with pleasure the introduction of the new dances—Continentals, Prince Imperials, Varieties, New York and Pinafore Lancers—in which the ladies and gentlemen acquitted themselves with skill and grace . . ." (December 25, 1880)

We can assume the musicians also must have performed with skill. New Orleans musicians took pride in being always able to play the latest dances, ordering music from Paris or New York.

Much has been made of the division between the colored citizens of the uptown and downtown parts of the city. The distinction has been greatly exaggerated. It was not due to any major dissension in perspective, it was merely the result of the difference of language. As the downtown French-speaking Creoles increasingly began to use the English language there was a more frequent mixing of the city's population. As an illustration, after an announcement of a dance to be given by the "Terpsichorean Social Circle" the *Louisianian* remarked:

". . . its membership is composed principally of young ladies and gentlemen of our French population, with a good sprinkling of our uptown gents. Success to them." (December 25, 1880)

A few weeks later, in a further observation on the same subject, the paper stated:

"It is with pleasure that American gentlemen notice the disposition on the part of the Creole young ladies to familiarize themselves with the English language. Conversation in the Anglo-Saxon tongue is not unusual in the 'elegant soirees' given in the fauburg." (February 12, 1881)

But in the Creole suburb, or "fauburg," it was still unusual enough to earn the attention of the newspaper's social column. As a people, the Creoles were probably the best educated in the South. They could have mastered the English language with ease had they so desired, indeed many of them did so as is evidenced by the Creole bi-lingual newspapers. An important reason why most Creoles, and particularly the Creole women, did not speak the "Anglo-Saxon tongue" was because that language barrier was used as a protective device against the predatory ravages of slavery. Creoles who spoke only French were more likely to be recognized as Free People of Color and therefore less likely to be kidnapped and sold into slavery. Moreover, their use as slaves would have been limited by their language "problem" and this would have tended to reduce the price kidnapers could demand for them. Creoles began to accept the English language only after the maturing of a generation that had not experienced slavery.

Earlier we touched briefly upon the romantic fiction of southern white authors who wrote of Creole women attending so-called "quadroon balls." Missing in those spurious accounts is the mention of language as a problem. Yet, as we see, Creole women did not feel secure enough to begin speaking English until a generation after the abolition of slavery. Even then the Creoles were careful to observe all the proprieties of their society:

"Tuesday of this week one of our third district social circles gave a complimentary picnic at one of our beautiful suburban parks. The uptown gallants were charmed with the pretty Creole belles, and enjoyed their little foreign peculiarities of speech and special forms of civilities. But the boys will put in their bill of complaint against the vigilant surveillance of the chaperons who are always in close attendance on these occasions, which tends to embarrass the bashful admirers of the Creole beauties." (June 25, 1881)

In a report of a parade and ball given by the "Young and True Friends" we learn the Excelsior Band is still led by Sylvester Decker, here spelled as Dexter:

"The True Friends assembled at Wesleyan Hall, on Liberty street, where the procession was formed, preceded by the Excelsior Cornet Band under the leadership of Professor S. S. Dexter. It marched to number 124 Franklin street, where Miss Filamin Delpit, a comely young Creole lady, presented on behalf of the Ladies True Friends Circle, a very pretty silk banner..." (February 12, 1881)

On February 19, 1881 the *Louisianian* remarked upon another social event at the uptown Cottrell's Hall:

"One of the most elegant entertainments of the season was given by the Camellia Social Circle, at Cottrell's Hall on First street last Wednesday night. The ladies wore very elegant toilets, the supper was par excellence."

This affair took place in the Bolden neighborhood, the Bolden family lived on First street for many years. It would seem reasonable to assume that in addition to the brass bands the young Buddy Bolden would more likely have been influenced by these "elegant entertainments" than by non-existent African dances in Congo Square.

Any rivalry between uptown and downtown citizens may have been more in the nature of which one could outdo the other in the elegance of their social affairs:

"The reception given by the Terpsichorean Social Circle was held on Monday evening February 21 at Economy Hall and was in every way a complete success, reflecting great credit upon the members. At an early hour the guests could be seen coming from all directions elegantly dressed. At 11 o'clock the spacious Hall presented a scene of unrivaled grandeur. The ladies were handsomely attired and the gentlemen wore evening dress. The entertainment was one of the most enjoyable given this season. The uptown girls have not equaled it for years." (February 26, 1881)

"The ball given by the Good Intent Social and Debating Club on Saturday April 13 was a financial success. Notwithstanding the inclement weather, the Hall was densely crowded with the elite of the Creole element. *Les Dames* came beautifully and tastefully attired in spring costumes, *Les messieurs* wore full evening dress. The entertainment was pleasant and enjoyable during he entire evening, for which the managers deserve credit." (April 30, 1881)

Social activity of both the Creoles and the colored uptown residents centered around balls during winter and picnics in the summer months:

"The Benevolent Daughters of Louisiana No. 2. commemorated their annual anniversary on Wednesday May 4 at Oakland Park, by treating their many friends to a fine and select picnic. Those who were present had a delightful and enjoyable

166

time. The music was par excellence surpassing in every particular any the writer has heard during the season..." (May 7, 1881)

A hazard of picnics was the occasional invasion of ruffians who attempted to crash the party:

"The picnic given by the Young Veterans on Thursday last at Oakland Park was a pleasant and enjoyable affair. The hoodlums absented themselves as usual. Their reception at entertainments given by the Young Veterans is never agreeable. Other Benevolent institutions should follow their example." (May 14, 1881)

Here is a notice of a picnic given by a downtown organization;

"The Jeunes Amis Association will give a grand picnic at the Magnolia Gardens on Monday May 30... This societe De Bienfaisence et d'Assistance Mutuelle is composed almost exclusively of our downtown Bon Tons, and is said to be one of the finest organizations in the city. Their contemplated picnic promises to be one of those grand affairs so characteristic of everything they have yet given; especially as, we learn, they have secured the celebrated Pickwick Brass Band, which discoursed such exquisite music at the Odd Fellows 10th of May Fair Grounds Picnic..." (May 28, 1881)

And here is another notice concerning an uptown association:

"The picnic given by the Hartford Benevolent Association on Monday June 13, was largely attended by the beauties of the Garden District... Dancing lasted until a very late hour..." (June 18, 1881)

There was a second dance hall close to the Bolden home as we see from this advertisement notice:

"A Grand entertainment tonight at Bell's Hall on First street... for the benefit of the Louisiana Rifles..." (July 9, 1881)

In a report of an entertainment given by the Knights of Athens at Loeper's Park, we learn the Excelsior Brass Band had its third leader in Professor Theogene Victor Baquet, father of

167

the famous clarinetists George and Achille. In this report once again it is made clear that New Orleans musicians were expected to play all kinds of music, or "music for all occasions." Here for the Knights of Athens the Excelsior Band played dance music, operatic selections, marching music, and music suitable for a serenade, all at one engagement:

"... The Excelsior Brass Band, under the direction of Professor T. V. Baquet, during the intervals of the dance, discoursed operatic selections from Fuhrbach, Balfe, Offenbach and Beethoven, which enraptured the guests with strains of music that caused many to pause in the grand promenade which encircled the spacious floor of the pavilion. Want of space prevents us from giving the programme of musical selections ... After the concert and dance the Knights repaired to the residence of Gen. R. B. Elliot and honored their distinguished guest with a serenade .. ." (August 20, 1881)

Interestingly, the *Louisianian* reporter noticed the "strains of music that caused many to pause." A situation to be repeated some fifty years later when the strains of swing music would cause many to pause from their dancing and linger around the bandstand, fascinated by the music. A week after the event for the Knights of Athens the Excelsior Band played a similar engagement at Loeper's Park, this time for the Americus Club:

"... As early as six o'clock sweet strains of music greeted the ear from the renowned Excelsior Brass Band under the able supervision of Professor Eugene Baquet and by eight o'clock a sea of faces had gathered and the Park presented a Grand Panorama of Venetian style and unparalleled grandeur. The La Belle Creoles and beautiful American ladies were blended together with such harmony and good taste ... Bye and bye the whole throng seemed to be in the giddy maze of the dance until the participants seemed forgetful of every care ..." (August 27, 1881)

Another report of this affair added:

"... The music under the direction of Professor T. V. Baquet was most excellent and comprised selections from the famous composers ... After the promenade concert the members of the Americus Club accompanied by the Excelsior Brass

Band tendered Hon. R. B. Elliot a serenade..."

The reference was to ex-congressman Robert B. Elliot of South Carolina.

The same issue of the *Louisianian* gave notice:

"The Pickwick Brass Band will celebrate its eighth anniversary by a complimentary concert and dance in the Pavilion over the Rhine at Spanish Fort today, from 4 o'clock p.m. until 11 p.m."

The "committee on reception" of this affair was named as C. F. Thomas, President; H. Hicks, Treasurer; H. C. Nichols, secretary; C. W. Flores, Musical Director. We can thus assume Flores was the leader of the band. Two weeks later the Pickwick Band again received mention:

"A promenade concert and ball will be given by the Pickwick Brass Band for the benefit of their relief fund on Saturday October 1st..." (September 10, 1881)

A few additional items from the *Louisianian* further illuminate the social environment of New Orleans during this period:

"Last Wednesday evening the Camellia Social Circle of the sixth District gave a reception to its guests. The entertainment was one of those happen-in-hops that are so agreeable among intimate friends. The Lancers and Varieties were danced to the strains of very good music. The ladies invited the guests to refreshments during the intervals. The Camellia deserve much praise for their efforts to please and entertain their friends." (October 29, 1881)

"The Mutual Benevolent Association of the Demoiselles de L'Avenir will give a Grand Calico Ball on Saturday, November 19th at the Equity Hall on Robertson street between Kerelec and Columbus streets..." (November 12, 1881)

"The Misses of the Golden Circle gave a soiree dansante at the residence of Mrs. Sarah Johnson, corner of Customhouse and Derbigny, Tuesday last." (November 12, 1881)

"The Troupe des Juenes Amateurs will give a grand concert at the Hall of the Amis de L'Orde, on Urquhart between St.

Bernard and Annette streets on Sunday, December 18th inst."
(December 3, 1881)

Several of the brass bands had members who doubled on
stringed instruments. The Excelsior was no exception:
"Tonight the Friends of Louisiana will give their Grand
Fancy Dress and Masquerade Ball at the Economy Hall. The
celebrated Excelsior String Band is engaged for the occasion . . ." (December 17, 1881)

About this time a new species of dance band materialized in
New Orleans—an event which was to have far-reaching conse-
quences.
The first dance bands in New Orleans were string bands
and from the mid-18th to the mid-19th centuries they were the
only type of dance bands in the city. With the appearance of
improved brass instruments New Orleans musicians were able
to adapt brass bands for the dance. Later when the improved
thirteen-keyed clarinet became available, particularly the type
developed by E. Albert of Brussels, a new hybrid sort of band
appeared consisting of brass, string, and woodwind instruments. Being without precedent, a mixed band of this category
did not have a name. New Orleans colored society, with typical
good humor, called it a "Tin Band":
"The Mid-Night Revellers have organized themselves into a
tin band . . ." (December 24, 1881)
Probably this group had been a string dance band but had
decided to include brass and woodwind instruments. This brief
notice in the *Louisianian* does not tell us just what instruments
the "Mid-Night Revellers" had in their band. We can be reasonably sure the band was led by a violinist who perhaps doubled
on cornet but we are left to speculate upon other instruments in
the band. Among the possibilities are flute, clarinet, trombone,
guitar, mandolin, and, for some engagements, perhaps a pianist.
However we can be sure there would not have been any drums
in this band. Drums were not added to the tin band until the
late 1890's.
If this array of instruments seems vaguely familiar it is
because here in 1881 we have our first documented evidence

170

establishing the existence of a type of band which, in the due course of its development, would eventually become known as a Jazz Band. This unprecedented grouping of instruments demonstrates, once again, how the New Orleans musicians were willing to experiment, to try new ways of producing music.

The people of New Orleans were accustomed to hearing either the soft music of string bands or the more sonorous sound of brass bands. To their ears this hybrid band had a "tinny" sound. Later, when these bands grew larger, they began to call themselves orchestras, but the nickname persisted. Even as late as the 1950s some older New Orleans brass band musicians still referred to this type of band as a tin band, indifferent to the fact that for several decades the world had called them jazz bands. Albert Warner, for example, the trombonist with the Eureka Brass Band, was fond of saying with some pride that he was a *brass* band, not a *tin* band musician.

To the ears of New Orleanians the tin band may not have sounded very mellifluous, still it had important advantages. Many of the older New Orleans dance halls, as we have observed, had constricted bandstands consisting of platforms or balconies inappropriate for large brass bands. The tin band was more suitable for these small halls, often being able to use the cramped area originally intended for the early string bands thus leaving more space for the dancers. As a small band it was considerably less expensive to hire than a brass band. On the summer outdoor jobs such as picnics the tin band had a superiority over the string band as it could generate a greater volume of sound, making itself heard over a larger dancing area.

It is interesting to conjecture how different the written history of jazz might have been if the early researchers had known more of the history of music in New Orleans. Had they sought to investigate the genealogy of tin bands instead of jazz bands, they may not have devised the African origin of jazz theory.

In New Orleans it was believed that a jazz band was a faker band. Not at all the same thing as a tin band which, despite its facetious name, was composed of skilled musicians. We have commented previously on the semantic problem in New Orleans. Jazz researchers from the academic world are unfamiliar with the New Orleans idiom, speaking what they have been taught to believe is "standard" English. New Orleans, on the other hand, is of a multi-ethnic, particularly French, lineage. The standard English used by the colored working people of the city, including the musicians, has similarities but is not identical to that of the ivory towers of learning. It is by no means certain which is the best or clearest variety. When researchers and jazz historians from the academic world asked about jazz bands in downtown New Orleans it was not realized by either party, the inquirer or the inquiree, that what was really sought was the history of tin bands. Because of this misunderstanding the attention of the researchers was directed to the uptown bands which, it was believed by some downtown musicians, were all faker bands. In particular Bolden's Band came under scrutiny, resulting in the situation previously discussed in Part One of this book.

Throughout the late 19th and early 20th centuries the tin bands, calling themselves orchestras, became popular. Ultimately they caused the demise of the string bands and restricted brass bands to street parades and funerals. The Silver Leaf String Band can serve as a typical example of the tin band development process. This well known band began adding instruments from its brass band namesake before 1890. About 1920, under the leadership of Johnny Predonce, it was reduced to six pieces, becoming defunct, along with many other bands, during the 1930s depression years.

In the 1880s however, brass bands and string bands were still the most widely accepted types of bands as we can observe in the following further excerpts from the *Louisianian*:

"Remember that the Economy Society will give a Grand Mask Ball tonight Saturday the 28th inst. in their Hall . . . Poncho Gayardo's celebrated String Band has been engaged for the occasion and a fine ball is anticipated." (January 28, 1882)

"The Young and True Friends B. A. will celebrate their second anniversary by a grand public installation and ball on Tuesday February 7th 1882. This sterling organization of the young men of the Third Ward will parade our principle thoroughfares

The six piece Silver Leaf dance band of the 1920's. Seated: Alf Williams, drums; Elmer Talbot, cornet; George Stewart, reeds; Clarence Tisdale, banjo. Standing: Albert Warner, trombone; Johnny Predonce, bass and leader.

The Silver Leaf was active as a string, tin and brass band from the 1880s to the 1930s. "Bat" Mosley continued the tradition using the bass drum with other bands, notably Kid Howard's brass band, into the 1960's.

during the day . . . The celebrated Pickwick Band is engaged."
(January 28, 1882)

"The members of the Economy Society will celebrate, by a
Grand Banquet, their 46th. Anniversary Wednesday March 1st.
at the Economy Hall . . . This is one of the oldest societies in this
city having a constitution and by-laws in every respect deserving commendation." (February 18, 1882)

"A Pleasant Sociable"

"Last Saturday evening the 18th inst. Artisan Hall on Derbigny street near Kerelec was the scene of one of the finest
social gatherings that it has been our pleasure to attend. The
occasion was the last entertainment prior to the Lenten season
of the Pinafore Circle. The Pinafore Circle is an organization
that was formed at the residence of Mr. John E. Staes, and was
organized principally for the purpose of social enjoyment. Its
membership is composed mainly of Creole ladies and Uptown
gents. Saturday evening the boys were out in full force, and they
are all unanimous in the opinion that for beauty and the select
character of the guests the entertainment was such that could
not be excelled . . ." (February 18, 1882)

"The Daughters of Louisiana No. 3 will give a Grand Fancy
Dress and Masquerade Ball on St. Joseph's night Saturday
March 18th 1882 at Violet Hall, corner Rampart and Common
street. Music will be furnished by Professor Poncho's celebrated
string band."

Here is a more detailed account of a serenade given for Governor Pinchback:

"A Serenade"

"Last Tuesday evening in the vicinity of Bienville, beyond
Claiborne, the beautiful calm which reigned in the stillness of
the small hours of a cloudless night, was greatly disturbed by
the silvery notes of melodious music. The Excelsior Silver Con-

net Band under the leadership of Professor T. V. Baquet, accompanied by a few intimate friends honored Governor Pinchback with the compliment of a serenade. The strains of music seemed to move the air as softly as a zephyr; in the neighborhood windows were raised and the lattice lightly touched. The Governor soon made his appearance on the porch of his residence and acknowledged the honor tendered him by his friends in the following facetious remarks:

'Gentlemen, for reasons best known to yourselves you have seen fit to disturb the peace and quiet of this orderly neighborhood with the sounds of excellent music and but for the fact that your purpose to do so was made known to me, I might find myself greatly embarrassed and utterly unable to command suitable words to express my thanks for the honor conferred by this mark of your respect and esteem. But just here, allow me to assure you that however pleasant it would be for me to indulge the flattering thought that you have tendered me this splendid compliment simply to gratify my personal feelings, candor compels me to confess that I do not place any such construction upon your actions.

You have chosen this course to manifest your approval of my appointment as surveyor of customs because you recognize in the act a disposition on the part of the present National Administration to accord to colored Republicans a fuller share of the honors and emoluments of the party than they have had accorded to them by former administrations.

Valuable and important in this respect, my appointment has a still greater significance which you have not failed to notice. It demonstrates that efficient party services, rendered often at the peril of a man's life is not to be held hereafter, when victories are won, as a disqualification for official preferment. It means that the National Republican party has returned to its cardinal principles and recognizes the equality before the law of all men, equal rights and exact justice for all classes of citizens...(After more in a similar vein)

...Gentlemen, it was my custom of old on occasions such as this to ask my friends in the house to "take something". I cannot afford to dispense with that custom on this occasion. You will therefore, please not stand in the order of your coming but

176

come in at once and let us see if we can find "something to take"'

The serenade party were cordially invited into the spacious parlours to enjoy the hospitality of the mansion. Toasts were made and happily responded to by Col. James Lewis, Messrs. W. E. Wilson, A. P. Albert and other gentlemen. While inside, the celebrated band enlivened the occasion by excellent selections of inspiring music. At a late hour the party retired in very hilarious spirits." (March 25, 1882)

New Orleans serenades were pleasant affairs and Pinchback, it seems, was not lacking in eloquence and hospitality.

In the casual manner typical of the *Louisianian* we are able to learn the name of another New Orleans brass band:

"A grand tournament and moonlight picnic will be given by the Hartford Benevolent Association on Saturday June 20 at the Oakland Riding Park . . . The Champion Brass Band is engaged for all night . . ." (May 27, 1882)

A fireworks display was a good excuse for music and dancing:

"A grand pyrotechnical exhibition and soiree dansante will be given by St. Joseph Young Men's Benevolent Association at the Delachaise Park, on Monday June 26th, 1882. This society never fails to draw a large number of its friends to its annual entertainments . . . The Excelsior Brass Band will discourse its choicest selections on this grand occasion . . ." (June 3, 1882)

The final issue of the *Louisianian* dated June 17, 1882 carried this notice:

"A Grand Picnic will be given by the Jeunes Amis Benevolent Association on Monday August 7, 1882 to celebrate their 15th anniversary . . ."

A brief announcement said the *Louisianian* would be incorporated into a newspaper called the *Protectionist*. Unhappily the files of this and several other newspapers published for the colored people of New Orleans do not seem to have been saved or have not yet been discovered. A situation which has also contributed to the historical silencing of the city's Black population

177

and the general lack of knowledge about their cultural environment and the music it created.

There were other Black-edited newspapers published in New Orleans, the files of which are only imperfectly preserved.

The *Black Republican* was a newspaper first published in New Orleans on April 15, 1885, only a few copies of which have been found. And a very limited number of issues of the *Republican Courier* for the years 1899 and 1900 have been saved.

Another New Orleans newspaper, the *Southern Republican* began publishing in 1898 but again a very small number of copies have come to light. A notice appeared in this paper on April 14, 1900:

"The Columbia Brass Band will make its first appearance before the public on Saturday evening April 28, when the band will give a Grand Prize Dancing Festival at the Friends of Hope Hall . . ."

The *Crusader*, a weekly paper mentioned by Desdunes, was the logical successor to the *Tribune*. Creoles were involved with this militant newspaper which began publishing in 1889. By that time the racists of the southern Democratic Party had consolidated their powers with the laws of segregation in full force. Most Republican politicians of the former Reconstruction governments had left for more fitting climes, but the Creoles continued their long struggle for democracy. Although it is believed more complete files may still exist, only one copy of the *Crusader* has so far been unearthed. This was number thirteen of volume two dated July 19, 1890. Even so, this solitary issue contains some pertinent items:

"The Friendship M. A. B. A. will give their first picnic on July 21, at Spanish Fort for the benefit of their Tomb fund. Dancing from 6 p.m. to 4 a.m. Music by the Excelsior Brass Band."

A meeting was reported of the Young Veterans at their hall on Marais street near Conti " . . . After the meeting the association headed by the Alliance Brass Band paraded the streets."

A further announcement said:

"The Co-operators Companions Debating Social Circle will give a grand festival and picnic at Loeper's Park Sunday August 31 . . . Music by the Excelsior Brass Band."

This copy of the *Crusader* also contained an interesting letter from the Excelsior Band:

"A Card"

"In the last issue of this valuable weekly we noticed the unfounded and false assertions of Equal Justice that the failure of their picnic was due to the Excelsior Band getting off the grounds and that we played only three times. We will say no greater falsehood could be uttered as we played two sets of dances from 7.30 to 10.30. We left the grounds because the chairman Mr. Milton Higdon, declared he would not be able to pay us after services rendered. Not wanting to play any more on credit for them, as they owe us $44, part of which over two years.

This information is given for the benefit of the various bands of the city, that they may look out for such bad payers.

Excelsior Brass Band"

The best known of the late 19th century newspapers published for the New Orleans Black population was the *Weekly Pelican*. With John L. Minor as the managing editor, this paper was published from December 1886 to November 1889. The social column, first headed "Rakings" later changed to "Notes About Town" contained many items of community interest patterned in a similar manner to those of the *Louisianian*. Brass bands receiving notice in the column from time to time were the Pickwick, Excelsior, Onward, Alliance, Oriental, Union, Pelican, and Brown's Brass Band of McDonoughville, one of the small towns across the river from New Orleans.

String bands mentioned were those of the Professors Martin, Duconge, T. V. Baquet, and Adolph J. Moret; also the string bands associated with brass bands such as the Union and the Onward. Our old friends the Big Four were still active but the personnel had changed since 1879. It had become formally titled "Professors A. L. Tio's and C. Doublet's Big Four String Band."[25]

Two bands not categorized were J. B. Humphrey's Crescent City Band and Dorsey's Band, possibly tin bands not yet recognized as orchestras, composed of excellent musicians but considered inferior in the quality of their sound to the brass and string bands.

Although most of the items in the social column of the *Peli-can* are similar in tenor to those of the *Louisianian*, a few are worthy of note. For example on December 11, 1886 the column suggested: "Why not have a grand ball, gentlemen of the Excelsior, Pickwick, Onward and Oriental brass bands?" Apparently four brass bands at one dance was not considered to be an excess of music.

On April 30, 1887 the *Pelican* announced:

"The Excelsior Brass Band of this city will leave the city about the middle of May for a six months tour through the North and East...They will have new uniforms made for sixteen men. They will visit Baltimore, Philadelphia, New York, Boston and other cities..."

Nothing further was said about this tour and as the social column continued to monitor the activities of the band within New Orleans in the issues of May 21, June 18, July 30, and August 29, it is clear the projected tour did not take place. Again we can speculate if this opportunity for the outside world to hear the New Orleans style of music in 1887 would have led to an entirely different written history of jazz.

Brass bands had become so numerous in the city that some parades were almost extravagant in their use. The *Pelican* for May 14, 1887 reported a parade of the Odd Fellows Masonic organization which was six blocks long and had ten brass bands.

The Longshoremen's Protective Union Benevolent Association, forerunner of the Longshoremen's Union, celebrated its 15th anniversary on June 4, 1887 with a parade led by the Onward Brass Band which, we are told, had thirteen pieces. And an orchestra of twenty-six musicians played at Spanish Fort, near Lake Ponchartrain, on June 22, 1889.

The *Pelican* expressly stated on October 5, 1889 that the Excelsior Brass Band was still under the leadership of Professor Baquet, but one month later on November 2, the paper reported a "subscription soiree" at the Amis Sinceres Hall with "Professor William Nickerson's Excelsior Brass Band". Nickerson, it seems, had become the fourth leader of the band. Baquet probably had decided to concentrate his efforts on the string dance band of the Excelsior which became known as Professor Baquet's String Band.

Another interesting article printed in the same issue of the *Pelican* contained the names of some famous New Orleans Creole musicians:

"The Lyre Musical Society"

"Last Sunday at the residence of Mr. O. Piron, 463 N. Claiborne street, the Lyre Musical Society was organized with the following officers: O. D. Pavageaux, president; August Pageau, vice president; G. V. Watts, financial secretary; C. Gulber, assistant secretary; O. Piron, treasurer; R. St. Cyr, first warden; Lino de la Rose, second warden; Mr. Lucien Augustin, musical director.

The object of the society is to encourage and perpetuate the art of music among its members. Among the prominent musicians present were Professors Louis and Lorenzo Tio [and] Baquet, Messers. R. Turnade, A. Page and F. Leclerc. After the meeting several classic pieces were skillfully executed. The society bids fair for the future."

*　　*　　*

The foregoing selection of notices from 19th century New Orleans newspapers, especially those owned and edited by Creole and Colored people published after the Civil War make it possible to glimpse a little of the long musical heritage of the city. These notices were concerned only with the more outstanding entertainments available. Undoubtedly for every one mentioned there were dozens of others which were not noted by the newspapers. Thus the Excelsior Band, recognized as the most popular of the Creole bands, received more attention in print than the many other bands playing concurrently in the city.

The musical heritage of New Orleans was a non-white—that is, Creole—heritage. During the period we have been discussing the only white musicians in the city were a few French musicians which accompanied the touring opera companies from France. Upon reaching New Orleans these were augmented by Creole musicians to form the orchestra that played in the downtown French Opera House; and in the 1890s and 1900s there were a few amateur immigrant brass bands playing music in the European style.

On July 7, 1856 when the *Daily Creole* described an Independence Day picnic where people "kept time to the music discoursed by the band in the merry dance" the music of New Orleans had undergone more than a century of development. The "art of music" which, in 1889, the Lyre Musical Society wished to encourage and perpetuate was not a new fad; it was an art with a unique tradition in New Orleans.

The era under discussion has been neglected or ignored by jazz historians. Partly that is the result of the silencing effect of slavery and Jim Crow racial segregation. In large part though, it is due to the red herring of the African origin fiction which diverted attention toward Africa and away from the social and musical history of New Orleans. But it is clear that by 1890, when Bolden was still a boy and ragtime music had not yet appeared upon the scene, New Orleans music for dancing, marching and for all occasions resulted from a distinguished and lengthy experience.

CHAPTER 13

PRINCIPLES OF NEW ORLEANS MUSIC

A music with such ancient lineage yet continuing enthusiastic public acceptance must surely have been based on enduring fundamental values. And those values were capable of being adapted for the use of string bands, brass bands and tin bands—the bands composed of brass, string and woodwind instruments. They could be applied to the performance of classical music, dance music, serenades, marching and funeral music. Yet they were flexible enough to adjust to the changing styles and fashions of music over a period of two centuries without losing popular appeal.

To describe those principles it is not necessary to become involved in technicalities. For those readers who understand written music there are many technical books available, for those who do not, such technicalities are merely a bore and are not needed here. Let it be simply stated at the outset that the principles of New Orleans music are not secret. They are the same principles upon which all European music is based and may be found in any standard method book. However they have been developed, adapted and expanded to suit the requirements of a unique social environment. An environment which existed for many years in New Orleans but had no parallel elsewhere.

This can be readily perceived by serious and unbiased researchers who have an appreciation of music and an understanding of New Orleans social history. Unfortunately in the past some authors of jazz books have had little knowledge of either subject, others have had a vested interest in continuing to adhere to the African origin theory. Often these writers have allowed themselves to become blinded to the evidence and to common sense in their obsession to link the music of New Orleans with the music of Africa. Thus we have been inundated with generally unintelligible jargon of African rhythms, call and response patterns and so forth. When musicians have attempted to contradict those essentially foolish assertions they have been subjected to derision, as witness the reception given to Morton's Library of Congress testimony.

It is patently absurd to suggest the music teachers of New Orleans—the highly respected professors who taught music to succeeding generations of New Orleans musicians—could believe such nonsense. The Professors Snaer, Davis, Tio, Baquet, Moret, Chaligney, Humphrey, Manetta, and so many others taught music in the accepted orthodox manner to generation after generation of New Orleans musicians. They used the same methods and method books used elsewhere either in France or America as is well known from many interviews with their pupils—the men who later in life were hailed as Jazzmen. These men were proud to have been students of the great professors to whom they gave much credit for their successful careers.[26]

One of the problems faced by authors writing on the subject of jazz has been their inability to distinguish between the parent form of New Orleans music and the derivative form of jazz, particularly dixieland jazz. Here we will try to draw some distinctions.

There can be no doubt the music that has become known as jazz originated in New Orleans. It should now be clear it came not from Africa but from a much older form of music that had prevailed and developed in the city over a long period of time. It is generally agreed jazz is based on improvising, or faking as it is usually called in New Orleans. A dictionary definition of improvisation is "playing without previous preparation". In New Orleans a musician's definition of faking would be "the playing of a person who cannot read music". These two definitions seem to be in accord, for a person who has not learned to read and understand written music would certainly appear to be playing without previous preparation. In view of this it seems reasonable to define jazz as "a sound produced from musical instruments which cannot properly be called music". New Orleans music, on the other hand, developed from and remains firmly based on the same principles that govern European music. This was the reason New Orleans musicians were able to play all kinds of music. Music for all occasions.

Again we may cite the evidence of Morton's Library of Congress testimony where Morton demonstrated blues, stomps, the Spanish tinge, Ragtime tunes, marches, dirges, popular songs, his own compositions including a tasteful example of what he termed "sweet jazz"—and Operatic arias such as La Miserere from Il Trovature.

We have seen that Creoles were artisans and music was always regarded by them as more of a craft or trade than a profession. As in all trades, various levels or degrees of skill were recognized. The most highly skilled were the Professors, usually proficient on several instruments, including piano, and generally thought to be the most qualified teachers of music. Next were the journeymen or "musicianers" expert reading musicians skilled in harmony and in variation, also considered capable teachers of music. These two categories were followed by the "readers" those who could play from written music but were incapable of creating variations. Regarded as semi-skilled were the slow readers, known as "spellers". Toward the lower end of the scale were the unskilled—the fakers, ear players or improvisers. At the bottom, the least skilled of all, were the blues players, the forerunners of some rock and roll and modern jazz players. Since all blues are merely variations upon one theme with a simple chord pattern, those fakers who could play only the blues were considered "one tune players".

It can be seen that in New Orleans as elsewhere in the music world, great importance is placed upon the ability to read music and understand the theory of music. This is not the situation in the jazz world, especially in dixieland jazz where an emphasis is placed on the ability to improvise, fake, or play by ear. Probably the only instance where a premium is put upon a lack of skill.

Improvisation has been so over-stressed that it is sometimes described as an essential ingredient in a progressive evolution, first of New Orleans jazz then dixieland jazz and on into modern jazz. This view is a total misconception. It is speculation without supportive evidence for the fact is that faking is a retrogressive movement *away* from the music of New Orleans. It

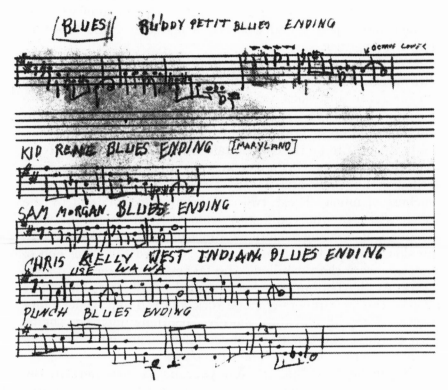

New Orleans musicians regarded all blues as simply variations of one tune. To personalize their blues playing the musicians used a distinctive final passage or musical signature. Depicted are the blues endings of prominent New Orleans band leaders in the 1920s. Notated by Punch Miller.

A 1960 photo of Punch Miller and Abby Foster the drummer with his 1920s New Orleans band.

would be more accurate to think of jazz improvisation as being a formula of style that stands alone, not closely connected to music of any kind. Certainly divergent from the principles of music that gave birth and sustenance to the New Orleans Style. One branch of that improvising formula gave rise to the early dixieland jazz and a variant of the same non-musical formula, a generation later, spawned modern improvisational jazz.

In the later version the emphasis upon faking is carried to an extreme degree. Even some performers capable of reading music take a perverse pride in being able to produce the utmost nonsense from a musical instrument. To a large extent the emphasis on improvisation has been encouraged by some jazz critics. Unaware of the protracted development period of American music their primary interest has been in the exploitation of "new sounds." The fact that those sounds were musically meaningless was considered of no significance. Since the approval of those critics was of importance in obtaining employment it is understandable that some musicians were ready to comply in producing endless musical absurdities. Perhaps it should not be so surprising that the machine age has produced an audience that can tolerate such grotesque travesties. In any event it should be made clear that the sounds generated in improvisational jazz have no evolutionary connection with the music of New Orleans, where the aim is to produce euphonious sounds, not dissonances seemingly tolerable only to the aurally impaired.

It is a cardinal principle of New Orleans music that, above all, music should sound pleasing to the ear. The musician is expected to have good intonation when playing his instrument. This is not so with jazz playing, where a good tone is not thought to have any significance.

In jazz it is considered poor form to play any music 'straight' or as written. The jazz player is expected to be faking or improvising at all times while playing. But the musicians of New Orleans believe any good melody can be pleasantly executed with little deviation from the written score. This should not be taken to mean that the musician is restrained from introducing variation whenever it is perceived to improve the music. New Orleans musicians played every type of music including classical music. It would follow logically that the musical principles on which European classical music is based would then be applied by those same musicians to other categories of music.

Variation, or thematic transformation, was used in European music more frequently in the past when the music of New Orleans was in its formative stage. As might be expected then, it comprises an important part of New Orleans music. Unfortunately variation is often confused with improvisation. The feeling seems to be that if a movement diverse from the theme is played from written music it can be called a variation, but if it is played without written notation then it must be improvisation. This generalization is part of the illogical thinking which has led to the unpleasant dead-end of improvisational jazz. It is far too broad and too simplistic. New Orleans music employs several modes of variation which can be applied singly or put into operation in simple or in complex combinations. They will work satisfactorily, however, only in a band that fully understands those principles of variation and can distinguish them from improvisation.

The forms of variation in New Orleans music are basically the same ones used in classical music although they are not always employed in exactly the same manner. Briefly described they are:

Melodic or Thematic—the melody is altered to a greater or lesser extent, or changed completely.

Tonal—changes in pitch or transposition of key.

Contrapuntal—counter melodies are introduced.

Harmonic—changes in harmony.

Instrumental—variations of orchestral arrangement.

Dynamic—changes in the volume of sound.

Ornamental—the music is adorned with fancy passages, trills, arpeggios, turns, and other decorative effects.

New Orleans musicians also experiment with meter and tempo variation if it is thought to improve the music; sometimes, for example, changing a waltz into 4/4 time or 2/4 into 6/8 time, or playing a tune at a faster or slower tempo than originally intended.

Lastly there is *Rhythmic* variation to be considered, which requires a more detailed description. One of the most distinctive features of New Orleans music is the emphasis placed upon rhythm—exactly as would be expected with a music designed to accompany dancing or marching. It is clearly impractical to vary the basic rhythm of such a functional music, but the musicians of New Orleans developed a way of bringing variation to the beat without disturbing the rhythmic foundation.

It is this innovation that has so mystified students of jazz and caused mistaken ideas of African rhythms. It was not recognized this effect was a new method of beat variation; instead attempts were made to analyse cross-rhythms and polyrhythms. The result was a false line of reasoning which led to a wrong conclusion. It was conjectured that since such rhythmic effects did not exist in conventional European music they must be derived from Africa. Those effects did not exist in African music either, despite diligent searching no one has yet been able to discover them, but this fact was then unknown and has since been disregarded.

Here again we can see how an imperfect knowledge relating to the long social history of the city led researchers to believe New Orleans musicians were jazzmen, fakers and improvisers playing without any real understanding of music. Some writers have unkindly suggested the musicians were drawing inspiration from "inner instincts" or "race memories" whatever those may be, thus perhaps unwittingly repeating the old "nigger music" racist theories of the culturally unenlightened slave and Jim Crow societies. It does not seem to have been seriously considered at any time that these original methods of enhancing the beauty and usefulness of music had been devised solely by the highly skilled and creative talents of a body of very practical and talented musicians. In America. In New Orleans. And without requiring assistance from European or African sources.

Older New Orleans musicians did not consider drums to be essential to the dance band. The New Orleans dance band existed for a very long time without drums, each member of the band being able to maintain a very danceable rhythm without drum-beats. Nevertheless a discussion on the subject of rhythm in the New Orleans style cannot now be separated from the use of drums.

We have observed how drums entered New Orleans music

by way of the brass bands and for at least a half century they were the only bands in the city to use drums. In the New Orleans brass bands the basic beat alternates from drum to cymbal, for example in 4/4 time it is marked by the bass drum on the first and third beat and by the cymbal, carried on the shell of the drum, on the second and fourth beat. The snare drummer is therefore free to embellish this rhythmic foundation with many fancy variations.[27]

With the later innovation of the mixed-instrument dance bands it was probably inevitable that drums would eventually be included. Perhaps a heavier beat was thought desirable to offset the heavier sound of the brass and woodwind instruments. But before the transition to drums could be made there was a delay of some twenty years. One advantage of the tin band was its small size; the inclusion of a snare drummer and a bass drummer would have made the band too large and too loud for some of the smaller dance halls. Pragmatic New Orleans musicians finally solved the problem with the invention of the bass-drum foot pedal. The original idea is usually credited to Didi Chandler who is believed to have designed and built the first model during the late 1890s.[28]

It is at this time therefore that drums first appeared in New Orleans dance bands. Not from Africa or from slaves or slave dancing but as a further logical step in the development of the tin band in the course of its expansion into the dance orchestra. The first models of the bass-drum foot pedal had the overhead type of beater used for about twenty years until replaced by the current floor model.

Although drums were a very late crossover from the brass bands to the dance bands they allowed for further diversity to be brought to the rhythm of dance music. A change of drum beats could be interposed into the basic rhythm as was done in the brass bands. The drummers of the dance bands were also drummers in the brass bands, they were able to bring their ideas for drum-beat variation into dance music. However, New Orleans musicians drew a distinction between skilled drum players and drum beaters; in dance music, it was thought, the drum playing should be "felt" rather than heard.

There are innumerable ways of introducing variation into

drum playing, each drummer has his own individual style and method. A noticeable example is the procedure sometimes known as "stop-time" although, strictly speaking, it is an incorrect term as the time or rhythm does not stop, there is only an interruption of the beats that mark the time. Other forms can range from the open break in which no beats are played through diverse modes of one, two, or three-beat combinations, to double time or shuffle rhythm. Another example is the Spanish tinge where a Latin beat is imposed upon the basic 4/4 meter. The objective of drum beat variation is to avoid the impression of a mechanical style of beat in the rhythm of the music.[29]

A dance band that can successfully employ rhythmic variation will add wings to the dancer's feet enabling them to dance all night without fatigue as generations of New Orleans dancers discovered. It was not unusual for a New Orleans dance orchestra to play a number for twenty minutes to half an hour. If it was received favorably an encore of the same tune would then be played for another ten or fifteen minutes, giving ample time for intricate variations to be fashioned. There are no reports of anyone becoming tired of hearing the same tune played over and over again. The reason, of course, is the variation brought to the tune. New Orleans musicians referred to their variations as "ideas," that is, ideas for variation, which prevented any tune from becoming repetitive or monotonous.

In any of its forms variation is used to beautify music. The rule is variation should add beauty, stimulate interest, be an aid to the dancers or marchers and be pleasing to the ear. Otherwise it should not be attempted. This concept is quite unlike improvisation which has none of those objectives.

New Orleans musicians believe it does not matter how poor a tune may sound in its original form, it can be made to sound beautiful by means of adding or substituting elegant variation. On the other hand a good tune can sound beautiful without variation if it is well played with good intonation. The creation of beauty in music may be considered as the heart of New Orleans music. It is the dominant motif. Unless this is understood it will be difficult for the novitiate to comprehend the philosophic difference between creating a variation for a specific purpose and merely faking an aimless improvisation.

Manifestly, developing musical beauty through variation, in a sense, ad hoc composition, is far beyond the capability of faker jazz bands. Being without knowledge of music they are restricted to simulating, as well as they can, sounds they have previously heard. For this reason a jazz band is an imitator band, one that primarily tries to copy the sounds, usually from recordings, made by bands composed of musicians. Regardless of how closely a record in the New Orleans style is copied, it can never be authentic simply because it *is* an imitation. Music must be original in concept, arrangement and variation or it is not New Orleans style. The faker bands of New Orleans usually hire one musician at a higher rate of pay so the band can learn new tunes and be able to respond to requests. A conspicuous example was the George Lewis Band, a faker band in which only the trumpet player was a musician. Although popular elsewhere, especially overseas, the musical qualities of this band were held in low esteem among New Orleans musicians. Ironically it was publicized as a New Orleans "traditional" band.[30]

The importance of originality in music was emphasized by the New Orleans social environment. With many bands competing for work, the choice jobs were obtained by those bands which had the most appealing, the most beautiful and the most original sound. Probably no two music bands had the same sound even though they played music within the same fundamental guidelines and often with similar instrumentation. This was well illustrated by the brass bands, each band having a style of its own. Early recordings of New Orleans bands also reveal this trait. The bands of Oliver, Morton, Piron, Russell, Noone and several others, were all music bands operating under the same guiding principles of music but each had an individual sound and used disparate orchestrations. Faker bands, however, have a similarity of sound to the point that one can scarcely be distinguished from another—a common complaint at Jazz Festivals.

Originality was also the goal of individual musicians, as each made a point of achieving a sound and a style unique to themselves. In this respect one of the most victimized of the New Orleans musicians has been the Creole cornetist Freddie Keppard. Among the constantly repeated fictions of jazz writing is the story of Keppard declining a recording session for the Victor Phonograph Company early in 1916 because of a fear of imitation.[31] At that time Freddie was on tour playing with the Original Creole Orchestra, managed not by Keppard but by Bill Johnson the bass player with the band. This group was remembered by Paul Howard as the finest band he ever heard.[32] The Creole musicians in the band were men far above having any diffidence about imitation, yet without corroborating evidence it has been repeatedly stated that Keppard refused to record on grounds of being copied. A figment which gained further impetus when it was discovered there had been a Victor test recording of a "Creole Jazz Band" on December 2, 1918. It was immediately assumed this was the same band associated with the unfounded Keppard tale, notwithstanding the story having expressly stated that Keppard prevented the band from recording and despite discrepancies of date, band title, and instrumentation.

As the Original Creole Orchestra had toured across the country for several years, playing before many thousands of people, there could be no logical reason to apprehend imitation. Indeed, the group was so talented it probably could not have been closely imitated. In the philosophy of the New Orleans musicians imitation is a sure sign of mediocrity, scarcely worthy of notice much less apprehension. Furthermore, the Original Creole Orchestra disbanded before December 1918 and so could not have been the band on the Victor test. Becoming sick in 1917, George Baquet the clarinetist, withdrew from the band in Philadelphia where he stayed for many years until, grievously ill, he returned to New Orleans. Shortly after, when Louis Nelson Delisle replaced him, the band broke up and dispersed.

Another fable involving Keppard supposes he covered his hand under a handkerchief while playing so others could not observe his fingering of the instrument. A ludicrous story for there is more than one method of manipulating the valves of a cornet and, of course, copying is done aurally. Ear players imitate sounds, not techniques.

Freddie is further maligned by repeated assertions that he was an unskilled faker, an improviser not a musician, despite his having played with first-class bands in New Orleans and Chicago. The Doc Cook orchestra for example, was known to have employed only skilled musicians and played from written scores. It is not possible here, nor is it the intention to detail or correct the many errors of conventional jazz histories, Keppard, however, deserves at least a few words said on his behalf to illustrate the distortions of jazz literature; also because as a man and a Creole as well as a musician he has been depicted inaccurately.

At one time there were a few brass bands in New Orleans composed of immigrant musicians. Among them the German bands were regarded as the most highly trained. These bands played classical music strictly as written in the European, not the New Orleans style; even so they were greatly admired for their excellent musicianship. Professor Manetta recalled he was relaxing at his home in Algiers one day when he heard the unmistakable sound of a German band playing classical music in a very fine manner. Intrigued by the superlative disciplined quality of the music, he strolled over to observe the band. "Imagine my surprise" Manetta chuckled, "When I saw my old friend Freddie Keppard playing cornet in the band". Here is proof that Keppard must have been a superior musician. The well schooled musicians of that German brass band would not have allowed a mediocre musician, certainly not a faker to come into their band and botch their music. Incidentally this is an early example of Creoles playing with white immigrant bands and shows the contempt many European immigrants had for the segregation laws of the South.

As another example of Freddie's ability, at the "Big 25" a downtown bar used as a gathering place for musicians, there was a semi-private room containing a piano. Here the two friends, Manetta and Keppard, softly played light classical music from the written score in duets of piano and cornet which were still fondly remembered by Manetta almost a half century later. From these and other similar stories and memories of contemporary musicians there can be no doubt that Keppard was a highly skilled Creole musician. He was able to play all kinds of music from classics to blues and was remembered by his peers as one of the finest cornetists in New Orleans. Because he was so greatly talented Fred Keppard may have aroused the envy of some not so gifted who then spread unflattering stories about him. It is hoped the preceding remarks will bring some balance to the subject.[33]

There is an impression in some quarters that jazz can be played only in 4/4 time. It may be true that fakers or jazz players cannot play in any other meter, but New Orleans music does not eschew any time signature. Dances in the city's cabarets, even as late as the 1950s, always included a few waltzes. Many musicians had fond memories of earlier dance meters such as the Mazurka or Quadrilles of several movements, each with a different meter.[34]

Although solos have always had a part in brass band music, older musicians agreed the smaller string bands and tin bands seldom used solos except as a simple variation. The musicians believed it was more important to play as a unit than as a collection of individuals and they used rehearsals to develop intelligent ensemble playing. Correct melody, harmony and rhythm played in co-ordination is more difficult to achieve than a succession of solos. Not only does it require a higher degree of skill but it allows for variation within the group. The excessive use of the solo is a prominent example of the retrogression of jazz from the music of New Orleans.

The counterpart of New Orleans style ensemble playing is known in jazz as collective improvisation. Collective or solo, the jazz improvisation consists of meaningless embellishment usually to the detriment of the original melody. Always played *forte*, this is the loud blatant sound Morton likened to a full glass of water that does not allow for any addition. In short, there is no consideration given for the use of dynamic variation. This results, inevitably, because the fundamental aim of striving to beautify the music, again a basic principle of New Orleans music, is unknown to jazz players. Ensemble variation and the playing of second and third harmony parts requires a degree of skill beyond the capability of jazz bands. Jazz improvisers, in New Orleans parlance, are said to be "readers of the green book" green being the color of naiveness.

The confusion about jazz evolving from African sources was caused by early investigators being unaware New Orleans music is founded upon the same principles that apply to European

196

music. Because of the historical silencing of Creole culture those researchers did not realize the music of New Orleans had a history extending back to 18th century France. In that long period of cultural semi-isolation the Creole musicians had built and expanded upon European music principles, producing a music suitable to a unique social environment existing on the American continent.

Social conditions in New Orleans were quite different from those prevailing either in Europe or elsewhere in America, so it should not be a source of wonder that the music reflected those differences. The early development achieved a revolution in the way music could be played. The change was so profound it was not recognized to be a development based on the principles of European music. The melodies, harmonies and rhythms of New Orleans music were unfamiliar and the variations were musically advanced beyond the understanding of ingenuous investigators. Those first inquirers were not aware the musicians were consciously using variation in a very advanced form. Their conclusion was that the musicians must be untrained or semi-trained and were simply improvising upon what the inquirers naively thought were strange—and therefore African—rhythms.

Generation after generation of the dancing population of the city, all colors and races, had no such illusions. They knew those rhythms to be eminently suited to the dance and were carefully crafted to lend wings to the feet. Combined with beautiful variations, the rhythms were so inspiring they enabled the people of "the Paris of America" to dance for hours or all night without undue fatigue.

The early researchers, although fascinated by the sounds of what they called jazz, were severely handicapped. They had no knowledge of the theory, principles or practice of New Orleans music, moreover they were completely unaware of the heritage and history of the New Orleans musicians. These first investigators were either conventionally schooled in classical music or had little musical experience of any sort. They were unfamiliar with the social environment which surrounded and nurtured New Orleans music. Since they were not historians, they were unacquainted with the fact that the importation of slaves to the United States was prohibited after 1807. In view of these disadvantages it is not surprising a theory was devised for the origin of jazz which, although presented in a persuasive manner and endlessly repeated by equally naive jazz writers, was totally erroneous.

Notes for Part III

1. Grace King, *New Orleans the Place and the People* (New York, 1895), p. 353.

2. *Daily Delta*, March 10, 1859.

3. *Daily Creole*, November 19, 1856.

4. *Weekly Pelican*, February 9 and April 6, 1889.

5. *A History of the Proceedings in the City of New Orleans on the Occasion of the Funeral Ceremonies in Honor of Calhoun, Clay and Webster which took place on Thursday December 9, 1852*. Printed at the Office of the Picayune 1853. New Orleans Public Library.

6. *Daily Creole*, September 1, 1856.

7 *Daily Delta*, March 10, 1859.

8. Leonard V. Huber and Guy T. Bernard, *To Glorious Immortality; The Rise and Fall of the Girod Street Cemetery*. New Orleans Public Library.

9. *Daily Delta*, July 14, 1856.

10. Eliza Kirsch. *Down Town New Orleans in the Early Eighties; Customs and Characters of Old Robertson Street and the Neighborhood*. New Orleans Public Library.

11. *The Louisianian*, April 29, 1882.

12. As with all other aspects of the segregated society, the Musicians Union in New Orleans was divided by race; Local 496 for Black musicians and Local 174 for White musicians. During the civil rights agitation of the 1960s the two Locals were merged.

13. *Daily Picayune*, February 27, 1838.

14. *Daily True Delta*, February 10, 1853.

15. *Daily Delta*, March 8, 1859.

16. The story of this incident provided by courtesy of Professor Manuel Manetta.

17. James Parton, *General Butler In New Orleans; A History of the Department of the Gulf*. (New York: Mason Bros. 1864), p. 517.

18. *New York Times*, September 29, 1862. Quoted in: Richard S. West,

Lincoln's Scapegoat General. (Cambridge, Mass. Houghton Mifflin Co. 1965).

19. *New Orleans Daily Picayune*, December 8, 1861.

20. "Pinchback, son of a white man, and himself indistinguishable from white in appearance, was born in Georgia, educated in Cincinnati, and had been a captain in the army." Cited from: W. E. B. Du Bois, *Black Reconstruction in America.* (New York: Harcourt, Brace, 1935), p. 469.

21. Dances held exclusively for children were a common feature of Creole society.

22. In reference to this man, Morton said: "Among some of the great pianists I may mention Sammy Davis, one of the greatest manipulators, I guess in the history of the world, on a piano. And a gentleman who had a lot of knowledge of music. He was a Creole, born and raised in New Orleans."
Speaking further of New Orleans pianists, Morton continued: "I have never known any pianists to come from any section of the world that would leave New Orleans victorious. We had so many different styles that whenever you came into New Orleans, it wouldn't make any difference if you came from Paris or any place in Europe, whatever the tunes were over there, they were the same tunes in New Orleans, because the boys always played every type of tune."—Jelly Roll Morton, *Library of Congress recordings*, 1938.

23. Before he contracted an illness that was to afflict him all his life, George Baquet was considered the finest clarinetist in New Orleans. His playing was so memorable that fifty years after the event, the clarinetist Emile Barnes said he could still "hear" in his mind the sound of Baquet's clarinet playing with the Excelsior Brass Band.

24. The Pickwick Brass Band and its successor, The Pacific Brass Band employed first class Algiers musicians including several members of the Manetta family. Cornetists Jules "Deuce" Manetta and Albert "Norm" Manetta played with both these bands. Later their nephew, Manuel Manetta, also played cornet with the Pacific Brass Band. In the early 1900s the personnel of the Pacific Brass Band consisted of: "Deuce" and "Norm" Manetta, Louis de Rooke, cornets; Buddy Johnson, Eddie Vinson, trombones; Joe Payanne, alto horn; Joe Leesard, tenor horn; George Simms, baritone horn; Albert "Dude" Gabriel, clarinet; Remeau, bass horn; Dude Simpson, snare drum; George Davis, bass drum. "Deuce" Manetta was the leader and solo E-flat cornetist.
For somber events such as funerals a regular brass band uniform was worn but for celebration parades some New Orleans brass bands featured flamboyant uniforms. The Pacific Brass Band wore a uniform of green, brown and gold and a green Stetson hat with a large white feather.

25. With the subsequent rise to popularity of the tin bands centered to a large extent around the newly improved clarinet the four members of the Tio family Lorenzo and Louis, seniors and juniors, became famous as clarinetists. Earlier however, the two senior musicians played violin with the string bands. The process occurred with other New Orleans musical familes. Louis Cottrell

snr. and Jean (John) Vigne were noted drummers but their sons, Louis jnr. and Sidney Vigne, became clarinetists. Professor T. V. Baquet led the Excelsior Brass Band as cornetist and the Excelsior string band as violinist yet his sons, George and Achille, played clarinet.

26. There may have been minor deviations from orthodox music instruction. Using the foot to keep time is an example, but that seems logical and natural in learning to play a functional music so emphatically rhythmic.

27. Snare drummer Baptiste "Bat" Mosley and his brother Edgar playing brass drum contrived a dazzling method of playing drum duets with the brass bands. When Edgar moved to California, "Bat" taught the technique to Chester Jones—a popular feature with Kid Howard's Brass Band. Unfortunately, as with so much of New Orleans music, it was never recorded or filmed.

28. This claim is not uncontested. Louis Cottrell jnr. believed his father designed and played an early bass drum foot pedal. Probably there were attempts made by several drummers. Chandler's model, however, seems to have proved the most successful.

29. Louis Armstrong's Hot Five, a studio recording group, and other similar small bands of the 1920s sometimes featured examples of beat variation on their records as an added novelty attraction.

30. As an example of improvising, the recording by the George Lewis Band given the title of *St. Phillip Street Breakdown* was really an attempt to play Woody Herman's *Chips Boogie Woogie* and Benny Goodman's *Gone With What Wind.*—Cited in: Martin Williams, *Jazz Masters Of New Orleans* (New York: Dacapo Press, 1978), p. 247.

31. First stated in *Jazzmen*. p. 22.

32. Paul Howard's Band, the "Quality Serenaders" made several recordings in 1929 and 1930. In conversation with the author Mr. Howard recalled his delighted astonishment when he first heard The Original Creole Orchestra at a rehearsal in Los Angeles.

33. Professor Manetta recalled that Keppard had a fondness for seventh chords, perhaps because he first played a stringed instrument—a common practice among Creole brass instrument players. In 1958, when cleaning out a closet at his home, Louis Keppard, Fred's brother, discovered the mandolin on which Freddie first studied music.

34. In his Library of Congress testimony of 1938, Morton demonstrated several figures of a Quadrille in various meters. As a further example, the author enjoyed Professor Manetta's rendition of music in nine thirty-two meter and his explanation of how, in New Orleans style, the beat should be sub-divided.

PART IV

THE LATER DEVELOPMENT

CHAPTER 14

THE ROLE OF THE DISTRICT

Because of its relationship with the history of jazz, the red-light District of New Orleans has become celebrated throughout the world. It is probably accurate to say the District has recieved more notoriety since its demise than it ever got during its twenty year existence. More widely known now by one of its nicknames—Storyville—this area was set aside for legalized prostitution from 1898 to 1917 under a city ordinance drafted by Alderman Story of the New Orleans city council. In the same manner as all other social activity in New Orleans during this period it was strictly segregated, intended for the use of white patrons only. Most New Orleanians simply called it "The District" or "The Downtown District" to distinguish it from other sections of the city where prostitution continued to flourish as usual, that is illegally, but for the most part ignored by the authorities.

Storyville encompassed thirteen city squares beyond the old city ramparts, which had become Rampart street, at the rear of the city where prostitution had thrived from the earliest days of the French colonial settlement. Story's ordinance simply legalized a de facto situation and in so doing made it possible for huge fortunes to be garnered by landlords, politicians and big-wig pimps. Previously the site had been allowed to deteriorate, contributing little revenue to the city. The passage of the new law dramatically reversed that situation. A building boom occurred throughout the area. Along Basin street, the main street of the District, large brothels were constructed, euphemistically called mansions.

The events leading to the official establishment of the District began many years earlier during the Civil War and were accelerated in the subsequent Reconstruction period. When

General Butler's Union troops occupied Confederate New Orleans in 1862 they were welcomed by the slave and Creole population but there was an immediate problem with southern white people, particularly the women. Some of these females expressed their dislike of the Union soldiers by insulting them and throwing objects at them from the balconies of their houses. To curb this activity General Butler issued his famous "woman order" which, in effect, decreed that any females found guilty of such unseemly behavior would be considered as harlots by the military court.

Order number 28 of the Department of the Gulf, promulgated on May 15, 1862, said:

"As the officers and soldiers of the United States have been subject to repeated insults from the Women (calling themselves Ladies) of New Orleans in return for the most scrupulous non-interference and courtesy on our part, it is ordered that hereafter when any female shall, by word, gesture, or movement, insult or show contempt for any officer or soldier of the United States she shall be regarded and held liable to be treated as a woman of the town plying her avocation."[1]

Butler's order achieved the desired result of ending the outward show of feminine rejection but it could not make southern white women become friendly to Union soldiers. If the lonely soldier sought the companionship of women he had no recourse but to visit the prostitution area where women were more concerned about the color of a soldier's money than the color of his uniform. As thousands of Union soldiers were billeted in or around New Orleans, business activity boomed in the District. With the increased demand for prostitution services there soon followed an increased supply of prostitutes and houses for prostitution. The red-light District began to expand in the only direction it could, further to the rear of the city toward the cemeteries where the colonial town had entombed its dead. When the Civil War ended New Orleans could boast of a red-light District second to none, by far the largest in the nation. So large that its activity had a noticeable impact on the economic health of the city.

Union troops were withdrawn at the close of the war but there was little slackening in the commerce of the District. The soldiers' patronage was replaced by returning ex-confederates and by northern carpetbaggers seeking to find their fortunes in the conquered South. Many of them probably attracted to New Orleans by stories of the District spread by Union soldiers on their return to civilian life.

But the greatest impulse for expansion in the District had yet to come. With the enactment of the Reconstruction programs the army returned to the South and to New Orleans. Not to exert its efforts fighting a war but as an occupying force. A peacetime army with much more liberty time available for the soldiers to visit the District on a more or less regular basis. And the troops were to remain in the South for some ten years. The District continued to grow as its fame spread and its population increased with an influx of prostitutes from all parts of the nation. These were good times for the District in more ways than one.

It was not until the late 1870s that the bubble burst. The ending of the Federal Reconstruction programs meant that once again the troops were withdrawn from New Orleans. This time the move was permanent, and with them went the northern fortune seekers. They left a sprawling red-light District over stocked with bawds and under supplied with customers for their wares. With so much competition for what commerce remained in New Orleans hard times descended on the District. The larger bagnios were obliged to release most of their staff and many smaller ones were forced to close their doors. But the prostitutes did not just disappear. They settled wherever they could find lodgings in the city and promptly resumed business. No longer confined to a specific area, prostitution became widespread throughout New Orleans. This led irate property owners to complain to city hall about the value of their property being depreciated by prostitution in the neighborhoods. The resurgence of the racist society, however, had changed the political climate. A different type of administration now held the reins of power.

Although viciously maligned the Reconstruction governments of the Republican party, city and state, had performed reasonably well under Federal protection. For example, Anton Dubuclet, a Creole of color, was appointed to the position of state treasurer from 1868 to 1879. When he was replaced by the southern Democratic party Jim Crow administration a committee of southern whites was immediately formed to examine his twelve year record of handling the finances of the State. It is easy to imagine the uproar that would have ensued had they found the smallest discrepancy in his bookkeeping. In point of fact, after a diligent inquiry of six months duration the committee was reluctantly forced to admit they could find no evidence of corruption; whereupon, instead of offering public congratulations to Dubuclet, the segregationist party in power quietly suppressed the report.[2]

In contrast to that excellent record the post-Reconstruction governments of Louisiana set new low standards for corrupt administration. The New Orleans *Mascot* of December 8, 1888 carried a front page cartoon suggesting in no uncertain terms that the city council had been conducting much of its official business not in council chambers but while ensconced in the local brothels. This factor by itself would not necessarily have further debased the quality of the council's efforts; compromises leading to legislation often can be reached at social gatherings, even in the parlors of Victorian-age whorehouses. Under those circumstances however, anti-prostitution legislation may have been difficult to achieve.

Alderman Story's solution was not original, the idea had been suggested several years earlier. It did not seek to legalize prostitution, the law simply made it illegal beyond a specified area. This stratagem avoided the issue of constitutionality that had frustrated previous efforts at legalization. Under Story's law authorities were able to move the white prostitutes from regions of the city where they were not welcome and relocate them inside the newly defined District. In other areas, for example the uptown colored District where prostitution presumably had always been illegal but not thought to be objectionable, the law was not enforced.

A rebuilding process took place in the red light District. Ramshackle dwellings, many dating from before the Civil War, were torn down to be replaced with ornate bagnios. A new method of draining the city by a pumping process enabled a modern sewage system to be installed which brought a novel

THE MASCOT.

PRICE 5 CENTS

VOLUME
3

NEW ORLEANS

Dec. 8, '88.

NUMBER
356.

SECRET SESSION OF THE CITY COUNCIL.
The Necessity of Another Belt Rail Road Amply Demonstrated.

The New Orleans Mascot of December 8, 1888 depicted the New Orleans city council meeting in a brothel.

The "Mansion" brothels in the 200 block of Basin street circa 1902. Lulu White's brothel in the foreground.

The same block viewed from the other end several years later.

Stalwarts of the red light district firehouse pose between two brothels. On the left is Emma Johnson's "Studio." At the corner is a house managed at various times by Mae Tuckerman, Julia Dean, and Wilamina "Willie" Barrera.

A souvenir postcard showed Basin Street circa 1910. All the buildings are brothels from Anderson's ground floor saloon on the left to Lulu White's three story brothel on the right. The railroad terminal is in the foreground.

(Upper) A Balloonist's 1912 overview of the District, and (Lower) of Basin street.

A 1923 photo showed a band and music stands on the balcony at the Temple Roof Gardens, the last of the large New Orleans dance halls. This hall served many displaced dancers after the District closed.

convenience to the District—indoor plumbing. The streets were paved and lighted, a firehouse built and reasonably competent, if corrupt, police service provided. All to ensure the big business of legal prostitution would be conducted in an efficient manner. Although it has not been possible to determine the financial arrangements of Storyville because the files have been vandalized, clearly large finances were made available for the venture.

The principle entrepreneur to operate within the revitalized District was Tom Anderson, a police informer who went on to become an oil businessman and politician. His commercial enterprises in and around Storyville included restaurants, bars, and at least two brothels. Because he was the premier pimp "Anderson County" became another nickname for the District. It is not always understood that prostitution, especially large scale prostitution, is a male dominated business. The opulent bordellos of Anderson County were operated under the names of their Madams, names that have since become famous—Josie Arlington, Lulu White, Emma Johnson, Hilma Burt, Gertrude Dix and several others but these women only managed the affairs of the houses. They were prostitutes, usually of a more mature age, promoted by wealthy pimps because of their ability to conduct orderly and profitable bordellos. The legalization of prostitution had the effect of also legalizing the occupation of pimp or "P. I." Financial matters were always firmly in the hands of these shadowy characters.[3]

In the large houses intended for the patronage of wealthy clientele an important source of income was the selling of champagne at an exorbitant price. Upon entering one of these "mansions" the "company" was greeted by a colored maid and ushered into one of several parlors or wine rooms. Here the customers were expected to buy drinks while appraising and conversing with the girls. The object of the house was to keep the "company" entertained—and buying costly drinks—for as long as possible before conducting the bedroom business upstairs. No amorous kissing, necking, or any kind of sex play was allowed at this stage of the proceeding. This was high class whoring, Victorian style, catering to the "respectable" bourgois. Supposedly discreet and certainly expensive.

In 1910, at the age of twenty-one, Manuel Manetta was

hired by George Kilshaw, the pimp of Lulu White's Mahogany Hall, as the regular pianist. This was the largest brothel in Storyville, staffed by light colored girls called Octoroons. Manetta had previously played at Willie Piazza's bordello, another Octoroon house, substituting for Alfred Wilson, the regular pianist, and apparently had made a good impression. His account of the parlor procedure contrasts sharply with fanciful published versions.

Manetta did not possess a singing voice; fortunately it was not required, as the girls were hired partly for their ability as singers and entertainers. Contrary to popular opinion they were not Creoles, they were well educated girls of light complexion imported from northern cities, a fact which was concealed from the southern white customers. Manetta was emphatic in saying Lulu White's girls were first-class entertainers with good singing voices capable of performing light classical songs in addition to the latest popular hits of the day. They were also expert at painlessly extracting hefty tips for themselves and the likable young professor who accompanied their performances. Manetta became quite a favorite with the girls. Lulu liked him so much she was fond of calling him "son" and on one occasion presented him with a ring containing a small diamond.[4]

The job of whorehouse piano player was not a salaried position; all money had to be earned in tips. As a consequence it was important for the musician to wear a suit with a vest, not for sartorial appearance but for the practical reason that it provided extra pockets to receive gratuities. Manetta enjoyed relating how each morning when he arrived home from the "night shift" at Lulu's he would empty his bulging pockets on his mother's kitchen table. And each morning when all his pockets were emptied the table would be covered with the tips he had earned, often including bills of large denomination. With the money obtained at Mahogany Hall Manetta was later able to purchase two residences in the suburb of Algiers. One for his mother and another for himself and his bride, in which he lived contentedly for the rest of his life.

Not all the brothels of Storyville were as elegant as Lulu White's fancy establishment. Some were famous for staged sex performances of various kinds, for example Emma Johnson's

"Studio" or "House of all Nations" in the next block of Basin street. In these houses the regular pianists were always female. If a male pianist was hired as an occasional substitute he would have to sit behind a screen, as Morton has described.[5]

Storyville was extremely profitable for about ten years but gradually as the novelty wore off and with the changing morals of society, business activity slackened. In 1908, to stimulate trade, it was decided to extend the tracks of the Southern Railroad along Basin Street and to build a new Terminal directly facing the largest brothels. Seemingly the city had no desire to have tourists wandering around town with loose cash in their pockets. Upon detraining male visitors were to be immediately presented with the opportunity of being fleeced in Anderson county.

To further expedite the process, guide books to the District were distributed in the Railroad Terminal. The most widely known of these booklets, the *Blue Book*, contained the names and addresses of all the girls in Storyville and pages advertising the services of the most prominent bordellos. The city authorities were very proud of their well conducted red-light District and were determined to exert every effort to continue the economic benefits it had brought to all concerned.

Despite these endeavors to revive the flagging commerce of the District, business continued to decline. If the District was to be saved it was realized some change in policy would be necessary.

There are few places on earth quieter than a red-light District in the daytime. This is the period when those who work the evening hours obtain their rest. All known photographs of Storyville invariably reveal deserted streets with only an occasional commercial vehicle quietly making deliveries of groceries and liquor to replenish the stocks of the houses. In Storyville the rule of quietness was strictly enforced not only during the day but also at night no loud disturbances were tolerated. Reports of brass bands playing at any time in the New Orleans downtown red light District may be confidently dismissed as figments of imagination. If a band were to approach the area too closely it would risk arrest. No dance halls were permitted and there were relatively few bars in which only piano music was allowed.

One of these bars was the Hundred and One (101) Ranch on Franklin street which, despite its grandiose name, was a small, sleazy bar patronized by small-time pimps, gamblers and regular habitues of the District. It was jointly owned and operated by an uneasy partnership of Billy Phillips, a southerner, and Harry Parker, originally from New York.

In 1910, as a further attempt to reverse Storyville's declining fortunes, a decision was made by city authorities to pursue a more liberal policy. It was decided to allow music and dancing in the hope of attracting more business. For several years there had been one or two colored bars, notably "The Big 25", just beyond the periphery of the District. Sometimes these bars had small bands that could be faintly heard at the 101 Ranch. Experimenting with the new policy, Parker hired a few of these musicians to play at the weekends. As this was not a steady job, the bands were really pick-up groups. No bandstand was provided, just a corner of the floor space cleared for the bands.

One of the groups to play at the 101 Ranch was led by Manuel Manetta who had lost his job at Lulu White's opulent whorehouse through a stroke of bad luck. He had decided to take a night off to see a prize fight, arranging for a substitute pianist, Louis Wade, to take his place. Unfortunately, Wade obtained access to a little too much alcohol and did not report for work, leaving Mahogany Hall without a piano player. Whereupon, in a fit of rage, George Kilshaw, the big-time pimp of Lulu's place, immediately fired Manetta.

The group formed by Manetta for the 101 Ranch had Jimmy Palao, violin; Willie Humphrey Snr., clarinet (later replaced by George Baquet); Eddie Dawson, guitar; John Vigne, drums; and Manetta at the piano. One evening Freddie Keppard visited the 101 Ranch with his cornet after playing a job elsewhere. Harry Parker told him to go ahead and play with the band. This precedent-setting incident was remembered by several musicians including Louis Keppard, Freddie's brother, as being the first time a cornet was played within the boundary of Storyville.

Primitive though it was, the impromptu arrangement at the 101 Ranch proved very popular. Most prostitutes in the District did not work in the large sumptiously furnished bagnios of Basin street. To the contrary, for the duration of their "shift" their business was conducted in small rented rooms called "cribs" containing just a bed, a chair and a washstand. The working conditions of these girls amounted to little more than semi-solitary confinement. Their isolation was further compounded by the fact that previously no females had been allowed to enter barrooms. With the District's change in policy the women were delighted to have a place where they could meet to talk with each other and dance with their pimps and other local habitues. Business at the 101 Ranch picked up considerably.

Sensing a business opportunity, Harry Parker quickly sold out his half share of the 101 Ranch to Phillips, who promptly renamed it as the 102 Ranch. Meanwhile, with financial backing, Parker proceeded to build an elaborate cabaret designed to take full advantage of the new liberal policy of Storyville.

Parker's new emporium, named the Tuxedo Cabaret, was in the same block as the 102 Ranch, a little further down Franklin street and on the opposite side. A large two-storied building, it was designed without a front door. After it opened in 1911 it remained open twenty four hours a day, seven days a week. The front was occupied by a long bar with a passageway at the side leading to the dance hall. At the rear of the hall there was a fairly wide bandstand about four feet high. Between the bandstand and the dance floor, in typical New Orleans cabaret style, there were rows of tables occupying a distance of about twelve feet, according to a newspaper report. Along both sides of the hall there were also tables where food and drinks were served. The upper floor was devoted entirely to prostitution. The Tuxedo Cabaret, in short, was a combination of bar, dance hall, cafe and brothel. Women were welcome and the girls from upstairs were freely allowed to mingle and dance with the customers when not on duty.

As a final added attraction, Parker wanted to be sure he hired a good dance band, so he contacted Manuel Manetta, the young man who had been so popular at Lulu White's elegant bordello and who had played for him at the 101 Ranch. Manetta selected a seven-piece orchestra with a nice blending of young musicians, older men and men in their prime:

Peter Bocage, violin.

Arnold Metoyer, cornet.

Louis "Papa" Tio, clarinet.

Gilbert "Bab" Frank, piccolo and flute.

George Filhe, trombone.

Louis Cottrell Snr., drums.

Manuel "Horse" Manetta, piano.

This was a band in the true Creole tradition, it was capable of playing any and all kinds of music. The popular music of that time was ragtime so this band concentrated much of its attention upon ragtime music.

There is an impression among some non-musicians, including many jazz critics, that ragtime music is "primitive" and easy to play. Those with a greater understanding need only study the sheet music to see that it takes a high degree of competence for ragtime music to be played properly. Ragtime is a stylized music not to be confused with "ragged music" which is a term applied to an inferior type of sound produced by fakers. The Tuxedo Band played rags as a major part of its normal repertoire but in New Orleans style with added, constantly changing, beautiful variations.[6]

Professor Manetta was a perfectionist in music; the "Master of all Instruments" and a veteran of various types of bands— brass, string, dance and concert. He was a man acknowledged by his peers to have been the most accomplished of all the New Orleans musicians of his generation. Yet he looked back on this Tuxedo Band with a certain fondness. We may be sure it was indeed a unique and superlative group.[7]

In a band of that type, specializing in the ragtime pianistic style, Manetta considered the bass clef figures could be managed effectively by his strong left hand at the piano buttressed occasionally by the trombone. The rhythm sufficiently emphasized to satisfy the needs of the dancers by the drumming of Louis Cottrell Snr. recognized as one of the finest of New Orleans drummers. Although pianos had been used with bands for years, so far as is known this was the first band of its type to substitute the piano for the guitar and bass fiddle. An innovation that was duly noted by the young white visitors to the

PHONE FO. 6-24

"Fess" M. Manetta

MASTER OF ALL INSTRUMENTS

.Ɔ LEBEOUF ST.   ALGIERS, LA.

Professor Manuel Manetta the "Master of all Instruments" demon-strates his remarkable embouchure and his ability to play melody on trumpet and harmony on trombone simultaneously. The trombone is secured around his neck by a saxophone strap.

Tuxedo Cabaret—the men who were later to become famous as dixieland jazz players.[8]

Here was a seven-piece band with three of the instruments—-trombone, piano and drums—that could be used for rhythmic variation and six voices that could also play melodic or harmonic variations. In practice only five instruments were so used. The violin, then considered an essential voice of a dance band, usually played the straight lead with only minor deviations. Acting as a sort of musical anchor it allowed the imaginative variations of the other instruments to depart, relate, and return to the melody and it kept the band from straying into constantly playing *forte*. Except for the first and last choruses the band usually played "beneath" the violin meaning, in Morton's words, that it played "soft, sweet and with plenty of rhythm."

The Tuxedo band was a "music" band as were all Creole bands. The members, with one exception, were "musicianers"—that is, journeymen musicians, excellent sight readers with good ideas for variation. The exception was Bab Frank the piccolo and flute player, older brother of Alcide who had been the regular violinist in the Bolden band. Unlike Alcide, Bab was a faker but he possessed a quick ear and was able to enhance the beauty of music switching from flute to piccolo, the highest pitched voice of the band, for tonal variation. Manetta said "he didn't spoil anything" probably the highest praise a faker could receive from the professor. Several older musicians believed Bab Frank to have been the originator, with his piccolo, of the famous solo in the tune *High Society*, further embellished and adapted for the clarinet by George Baquet and finally popularized by Alphonse Picou after Baquet left the city.

The highly competent group of musicians at the Tuxedo did not hesitate to play difficult numbers. Soon it achieved a reputation among New Orleans musicians—notoriously stern critics of music. There were several extra chairs at the rear of the bandstand available for any musicians who wanted to "sit in" with the band. Parker had learned from his days at the 101 Ranch that Creole musicians enjoyed visiting and playing with each other. As a Northerner he was much less racially prejudiced, leaving the band to handle its own affairs. As a businessman he had no objection to having extra musicians which he did not need to pay. There is even some evidence he had an appreciation of music, taking pride in having the best band in Storyville. Not regarding them as simply a "nigger band" in the typical boorish manner of the segregated society.

At the Tuxedo the band played from 8:00 p.m. until 4:00 a.m. an hour or two later than most jobs, so musicians often visited to play with the band when their own work had ended. When playing late jobs in the days before the automobile many musicians did not travel home until daylight fearing hold ups, muggings or worse. An apprehension well justified in the racially divided city. Several bars "for colored" were open all night where musicians could await the dawn and the morning street cars, but spending a little time calling upon and playing with another band was considered preferable to merely sitting in a bar. In due course a large number of musicians sat in and played with the Tuxedo Band.

One of the band's visitors was the clarinetist Sam Dutrey, acknowledged as a severe critic of music and musicians and older brother of the better known Honore "Nora" Dutrey, trombonist on the first Joe "King" Oliver records.[9] Taking a seat behind Frank one evening at the Tuxedo, Sam noticed the sheet music on Bab's music stand was upside down. At the close of the evening Parker, apparently aware of Dutrey's reputation as a critic, strolled up to ask Sam: "Well, how do you like the band?"

"It's a pretty good band" Sam conceded, "All except that man there" pointing to the embarrassed Bab and causing the band to have a good laugh at Bab's expense.

A few years later Sam Dutrey was playing in another Manetta band when the cornet player became ill. The cornetist contacted Manetta to say he was sending the young Louis Armstrong to play as his substitute. When the band arrived on the job "Little Louis" as he was then known, was sitting on the bandstand.

"Get off that stand, boy" roared Sam, scaring Louis half to death. Manetta intervened, saying Louis was going to play with the band.

Sam would have none of it. "That kid can't play with the

band, he will only mess up the music."

"Well at least give him a try-out" reasoned Manetta, who had known Armstrong from the days when, as Joe Oliver's protege, Louis had been around the Ory-Oliver Band in which Manetta was the pianist.

The band stomped off with Louis on his best behavior, playing within the normal range of his instrument being careful not to trespass or trample upon Sam's clarinet part. At that time Louis was using a cornet with a deep-cup mouthpiece; it was not until he reached Chicago that he became a "high note screamer" when he changed to a trumpet with a shallow-cupped mouthpiece. Knowing he was on trial "Little Louis" gave it everything, playing as he had never played before and perhaps never did again.

At the close of the number Manetta, keeping a straight face, turned to Sam: "How did he do?"

Reluctantly Sam grunted "He can stay."

And the band, which had been almost bursting, exploded into laughter, this time at Dutrey's expense.[10]

Playing music New Orleans style is not an easy job, perhaps that is one reason why so few can do it successfully. It is hard work that requires an occasional wetting of the whistle. The members of the Tuxedo Band usually brought a half-pint bottle of whisky to work as an aid to their spirits during the long hours of the evening. Sunny Brook whisky was the preferred brand at twenty-five cents the half pint. When musicians came around to sit in they also brought "a little taste" for the band. The empty bottles were stacked conveniently behind the piano. After a week or two, perhaps during the playing of a boisterous ragtime stomp when the piano shook with enthusiasm, discordant sounds could be heard as the heap of bottles subsided. This was the signal for the practical and frugal nature of Manetta to assert itself. The next afternoon he gathered the empty bottles and returned them to the store. In those days each bottle carried a small redeemable deposit. In exchange for many empty bottles he returned with a few full ones, ready to start a new pile behind the piano.

Arnold Metoyer left the Tuxedo band after a year or so to lead a band of his own. Finding a man to replace him was a difficult decision for Manetta. Metoyer was a first-rate Creole cornetist, a man ranked with such Creole luminaries as Fred Keppard and Manuel Perez. With some misgivings Manetta was persuaded to hire Oscar Celestin but he was never completely satisfied with his choice. Celestin was a reader of music and therefore capable of playing the "book" of the band which included some difficult numbers and many ragtime tunes. But he was not a "musicianer" in the sense of having "ideas"; of being able to create and embellish the beautiful variations for which the band had become renowned. Often the other musicians had to support or "carry" him. Even so, the fact that he had played with the famous band at the Tuxedo Cabaret enabled Celestin to build his career. After the Tuxedo Cabaret closed Celestin led several bands using a second cornet player which he labeled as the Tuxedo Band.[11]

Over the years there were a number of Tuxedo Orchestras and Tuxedo Brass Bands. Indeed the name of the Tuxedo Band was so illustrious that fifty years after Storyville became history there was still a "Young Tuxedo" Brass Band in New Orleans led by John Casimir, a clarinetist pupil of Manetta. It is a tribute to the magnanimous nature of the Professor that he never objected to others using the name of his true, original, Tuxedo Band.

The huge success of the Tuxedo Cabaret drew business away from the 102 Ranch, further exacerbating the ill feeling between Parker and Phillips, the ex-partners of the 101 Ranch. On Monday, March 24, 1913, a shooting fracas erupted in the Tuxedo bar which left both Phillips and Parker dead of gunshot wounds. No musicians were present and although there was much speculation, the exact details of the affair were never determined nor was anyone brought to trial. The resulting public media outcry caused the closing of all the cabarets in Storyville for several months although the brothels remained open. In the course of reporting the shooting, the *Daily Picayune* newspaper for March 25, 1913, gave the following description of the Tuxedo dance hall:

"This is a large hall possibly 100 feet in length and about 30 or 40 feet wide. At the lower end of the hall a stand has been erected for the music . . . Here a Negro band holds forth and from about 8 o'clock at night until 4 o'clock in the morning plays varied rags, conspicuous for being the latest in popular music, interspersed with compositions by the musicians themselves. The band has a leader who grotesquely prompts the various pieces . . .

The leader of the band at the Tuxedo was the pride of the house. Harry Lauder, Billy Van or George Evans never had anything on him in fancy facial expressions or funny tricks of the legs. When he led the band people stopped to watch his antics. He was probably the only salaried man in the band, the others being supported by tips they received from the dancers . . ."

This entertainer, of course, was not the leader or a member of the band. Manetta remembered him as an itinerant entertainer allowed in the hall by Parker to dance, gesticulate and otherwise amuse the customers. The reporter was equally confused in the matter of tips and salary. Itinerant entertainers depended entirely on the tips they were able to solicit. The band received a retainer salary although, as with most enterprises in the District, they were expected to be supported in part by tips.

When the cabarets of Storyville were allowed to resume business the Tuxedo, under new management, was renamed. It was called the Villa Cabaret in an effort to avoid any stigma the Tuxedo name may have acquired because of the shootings. Manetta again formed the band retaining Bocage and Frank and adding Joe Howard, cornet; Eddie Atkins, trombone; Lewis James, clarinet; and Baby Dodds, drums. Later Manetta led other bands in the area. At Rice's Cabaret, for example, with Ezab "Zeb" Lenares, a notable New Orleans clarinetist, and Ernest "Ninnez" Trepagnier another of the legendary New Orleans drummers. Manetta gave Trepagnier the nickname of "Quank" because of the loud duck call which Trepagnier blew during the otherwise open breaks of the music. In those less industrialized times animal sounds from the band were popular crowd pleasers.[12]

There were other cabarets in and around Storyville where music could be heard. The final edition of the District's direc-

226

tory, the *Blue Book*, listed nine cabarets. Four of them, two for whites and two for colored, were not within the borders of the District. They were:

The Casino Cabaret (white) 1400 Iberville street.

The Union Cabaret (white) 135 North Basin street.

Lala Cabaret (colored) 135 North Franklin street.

New Manhatten Cabaret (colored) 1500 Iberville street.

In 1917 when the District was closed by order of the Navy Department, only five cabarets were affected, all restricted for the use of white people:

Abadie Cabaret, 1501 Bienville street.

102 Ranch, 206-208 North Franklin street.

My Place Cabaret, 1216 Bienville street.

Villa Cabaret, 221 North Franklin street.

Rice's Cafe and Cabaret, 1501 Iberville street.

As some of these places had music at the weekends only, it is probable that a total of less than two dozen musicians lost full time employment.

The episode of Storyville had involved band music for no more than six or seven years. It was not a major part of the music scene in New Orleans and its closure was not a serious set back for musicians. The majority of them had never been employed in Storyville and so did not miss it as a source of employment. Certainly the termination of the District did not trigger a mass departure of musicians to Chicago and California as is frequently asserted in conventional jazz books. The first World War had induced many southern Black people to seek work in northern factories. It could be expected there would be those musicians who would also seek potentially greener pastures in the North. Probably a more compelling reason to leave New Orleans was the rise to popularity of the white dixieland bands which began to seriously limit the amount of work available for the colored bands.

Musicians who went to Chicago did not travel by riverboat, as is often stated; they went by train which was considerably faster and less expensive. Those musicians who worked on the boats did not leave their employment in northern ports of call. They signed contracts for the complete summer season and were not paid their full salary until the season's work ended in the fall. It is worth noting that the major riverboat owners, the Strekfus family, could have had their choice of musicians throughout the length of the Mississippi River, yet they chose colored musicians from New Orleans.

In Chicago a comparatively few New Orleans musicians achieved a measure of success, but many of those men who went North did not stay long. Some became homesick, others could not find sufficient work and still others did not care for the climate and decided to return home.

The downtown red-light District was segregated for the use of white customers only. A controlled number of Black and Octoroon prostitutes were permitted and a few colored maid servants were employed in the larger bagnios, but for Black people in general and Black men in particular the area was strictly forbidden territory. The fact is, Storyville's existence and eventual extinction was a matter of indifference for the Black community as a whole. However, if the District had little influence upon New Orleans music, it did have a great deal to do with the origin of a type of music subsequently to become known as dixieland jazz.

CHAPTER 15

DIXIELAND JAZZ

It is reasonable and pertinent to ask why colored bands were employed in Storyville under its liberalized entertainment policy. The downtown District was off limits to members of the colored population, they were subject to immediate arrest if they were found inside the boundaries without a good excuse. Given the extremely racist attitude then prevalent if there had been an alternative available it is certain that "nigger bands" as they were commonly called by southern whites, would not have been chosen to play their "nigger music" in the prostitution area reserved for "white folk."

The only logical answer to the question must be that there was no alternative. Dance bands consisting of white musicians simply did not exist in New Orleans. Nor had they ever existed at any time in the long history of music and dancing in the city. This was common knowledge with all the older musicians of New Orleans, but the mute testimony of Storyville proves the point convincingly.[13]

Although this glaring evidence is prominent for serious researchers and historians to observe it has seldom been mentioned, still less emphasized, in any of the innumerable books and articles dealing with the origin of jazz or the history of music in New Orleans. The thunderous silence should not surprise us. Historians are also human; they are seldom able to escape from their own prejudices and that has always been particularly true of southern historians.

Indisputably colored musicians did play music in Storyville, the evidential data is overwhelming. Many musicians have testified of their experiences in the District. As has been noted, a white-owned and operated New Orleans newspaper, the *Picayune,* reported on the presence of a "Negro band" at the

Tuxedo Dance Hall. This was really Professor Manuel Manetta's band of Creole musicianers, but such fine distinctions could not be expected of the *Picayune*.

Playing music for white people was nothing new for Creole musicians. They had supplied music for all the New Orleans population over a period of several generations. They had attended the most prestigious official affairs; they had played for parades, on the riverboats and in dance halls; for excursions, concerts and private parties. And they had provided music for the baptismals, marriages, anniversaries and deaths of both races.

It is true that by 1911, when music for dancing was first allowed in Storyville, there were a few non-Creole uptown bands, and some Creole bands contained a few uptown musicians. It is also true there were Creoles who resided uptown or in Algiers and other suburbs as the residential population became increasingly homogeneous but there were no bands of white musicians. Creole bands were still recognized as the finest, and they continued to be the main providers of music in the city.

It is essential to note, however, that at about this time the music situation in New Orleans was beginning to change as the whole social environment of the city was undergoing a fundamental and far-reaching transition.

When slavery was abolished in New Orleans it set the wheels into motion for a social revolution in the embodiment of the labor force. Previously white persons had been able to buy slaves and live on the product of their labor. Frequently, though, urban slaves became part of a more informal relationship. In return for the protection of a white master, usually consisting of a "pass" or ownership paper that would be accepted as valid by the police, the slaves shared their remuneration or the profits of their enterprise with the "master." This system had benefits, of a sort, for both master and slave. The slave was afforded protection from predatory practices and was able to keep a little money for himself. The master was not required to buy, feed, clothe and house the slave. In short, the master was reduced to a species of pimp, another demoralizing effect of slavery.

The protection of a white master was of vital importance to

an urban slave. Without it he was liable to be arrested or kidnapped and sold to labor on a plantation. There he would have to work in the fields from dawn to dark—that is, from the time when people can see to work until the time when they cannot. Or "Kin to Kant" as it was known.[14] As a field worker he could suffer brutality or death at the whim of the owner or his slave drivers. With protection, however, an urban slave could enjoy a small measure of independence. For example, it was common for slaves equipped with handcarts to obtain produce from the local markets which, as street hawkers, they then sold to neighborhood households.

With the abolition of slavery a master's protection was no longer needed, an ex-slave could keep all his remuneration or profits for himself.

In theory.

In practice such social changes did not occur overnight. Very unpleasant things could happen to an ex-slave who tried to escape the clutches of his master. White ruffians, probably former slave drivers on the same order as the Ku Klux Klan, were employed as "enforcers" for ex-slaves who became too independently minded.

It is only in the pages of the Black-owned newspapers that we see evidence of the enforcement procedure. The *Louisianian* for October 1, 1871 in reference to this matter wrote:

". . . We have so frequently dwelt of late on such disgraces to our community, so often deplored the lax public sentiment on so grave a question, that it is useless for us today to do more than keep our readers informed of these atrocious things, in the hope that the very horror of the cases will produce such a revulsion of popular feeling on the murder question as will demand not only the swiftest and the sternest, the most inflexible administration of justice on the part of our criminal courts, but will also elevate the common estimate of human life . . ."

Gradually, as time passed and a new generation which had not experienced slavery came of age, social conditions began to change. The process was hastened by the large influx of immigrants during the late nineteenth century. Increasingly white people entered the labor market, as a result Black workers were dispossessed of their jobs, sinking ever lower down the economic scale. One after another occupations and crafts were usurped by white workers until, in the course of several decades, the labor force changed from almost totally Black to almost totally white. Black workers were restricted to work within the Black community or were relegated to the most menial positions of labor. Finally, during the depression of the 1930s, even the street cleaners and trash collectors of the city were replaced by white workers, thus marking the completion of a sixty-year cycle in the composition of labor.

Music was by no means immune to this change in social conditions. Young white boys, well aware they faced the necessity of earning a living, listened to the music of the Creole brass bands on the streets and were inspired to reproduce those intriguing sounds as a means of employment. There is some evidence to indicate that the children of immigrants whose parents had musical experience in Europe were particularly influenced. Perhaps because they heard their parent's remarks relating to the novel and superior quality of Creole music, and they realized there was really no color stigma attached to the playing of music since their parents had done so.

But where could these children learn how to play such wonderful music? Most of them were from poor families who could not afford music lessons. Some parents would not have approved of their progeny seeking instruction from colored teachers, others had higher ambitions for their offspring than the playing of "nigger music", for in those years it was of vital importance to avoid acquiring the epithet of "nigger lover". Consequently most of those white children who were determined to play music did so as fakers.

It is generally believed the process of encouraging white boys in their music and eventually organizing them into bands began with Jack Laine about 1905. Jack had a blacksmith shop which became a gathering place for schoolboys when his sons, who were interested in music, brought their friends around to try out their instruments. A blacksmith shop might seem an unlikely setting for schoolboy fakers to rehearse music, but it appears this was exactly the sort of environment that would serve as a springboard for adolescent ideas. Loud, often discordant sounds emanating from a blacksmith shop would not be considered too unusual, enabling the juveniles to practice together with no outside interference or neighborhood complaints. The boys were also fortunate in receiving assistance from two young Creole musicians light enough in color to be accepted as white—Dave Perkins, who later became a music teacher, and Achille Baquet, youngest son of Professor T. V. Baquet.

Soon, as word spread among the youths, Laine was able to form first one and then several "kid bands." These were patterned along similar lines to the Creole brass bands which the boys had observed on the streets. One of Laine's sons, Alfred, born in 1895, eventually became a cornet player in a band managed by his father.

The quality of music produced by these bands of youthful fakers left much to be desired. Their attempts to imitate the great Creole brass bands were admittedly weak, but the boys had other factors in their favor. Foremost was the obvious fact they possessed white skin. In the racist society it was to be expected there would be those white people who resented having to hire colored bands. Since most southern racists, almost by definition, had little knowledge or appreciation of music, the inferior quality of these juvenile bands was of no concern. It was music played by white musicians and therefore preferred. Also the musicians were youthful and for that reason to be encouraged.

Jack Laine was not slow to realize these advantages. He appears to have been a competent manager, obtaining sufficient work for his boys to keep them busy. Before long he was able to abandon his blacksmith work to become a full-time booking agent. Because he was so successful in his efforts to organize and obtain employment for these boys, some of whom later achieved fame as members of dixieland jazz bands, Laine was called the father of dixieland jazz. But in his senior years, he lived to the age of ninety-three, Laine looked back on that time as a relatively unimportant part of his life, occupying only about a dozen years. With the onset of the first World War he retired from the music world to occupy himself with other endeavors. [15]

Meanwhile his boys were growing into young men. A few of them had acquired a knowledge of music, becoming readers or learning enough to qualify as spellers. Of these, some had attended colored teachers. Usually we know of it only from their teachers or fellow students. For example, Emmett Hardy, a talented cornet player who is supposed to have influenced Bix Beiderbecke, was a student of Professor Manetta; Jack Teagarden, originally from Texas, took lessons from Vic Gaspard at the same time as Eddie Summers. But most of Jack Laine's youthful brood continued to rely upon their ears, listening to the Creole brass bands on the street and trying to imitate them as well as they could. There were limitations to this process. White boys did not care to follow the bands, or "second line" in the colored neighborhoods so their listening time was usually quite short. With such restrictions it was not always easy to remember what they had heard, at least not sufficiently well to copy it in a satisfactory manner. Laine's bands had a very limited repertoire consisting of tunes made up from parts of the music they had heard colored bands play. The youngsters did not know the correct names of the tunes as they did not fraternize with colored musicians, anyway the mishmash of sound would probably have been unrecognizable. To identify their "make up" music the boys used "make up" names or numbers, or sometimes a combination of both. One of their most popular tunes was given the title of *"Nigger Number Two".* [16]

When Storyville adopted the policy of permitting cabarets with band music some of Laine's young men were old enough to enter the District without having the police chase them out. Here it was possible for the young men to listen to New Orleans dance music night after night over an extended period of time. For the price of a sandwich and coffee or a couple of drinks they were able to stay in the cabarets for hours soaking up the exhilarating sounds. It is interesting to note the ages of some of the future Dixielanders in 1911 when the cabarets of the District were permitted to employ music.

The first white dixieland band departed New Orleans in

1915 to play in Chicago. This was called Tom Brown's Band from Dixieland. The members of the band and their ages were:

Name	Age in 1911
Tom Brown	23
Ray Lopez	22
Arnold Loyacano	22
Billy Lambert	18
Gussie Mueller	21

The second New Orleans white band to go to Chicago, in 1916, was Johnny Stein's Band which, without Stein, later became famous as The Original Dixieland Jazz Band. The personnel of this band was:

Name	Age in 1911
Johnny Stein	20
Nick LaRocca	22
Eddie Edwards	20
Henry Ragas	20
Alcide Nunez	19
(Nunez was later replaced by)	
Larry Shields	18

It can be seen these young men were old enough to enter the newly opened cabarets of Storyville. They became regular visitors to the several bands then playing in the District. Later, when they had become famous as players in dixieland bands, Manetta recalled their presence in the District and meeting some of them at the Tuxedo Cabaret. He especially remembered Nick LaRocca, although LaRocca is not known to have given any credit to the colored musicians.[17]

It should not be thought all the Dixielanders were equally as ungracious in acknowledging their debt to the New Orleans musicians. Most of them privately agreed whatever success they attained in the world of music was due to the help and inspiration they received from the colored musicians. Dixieland band leaders Tom Brown and Albert "Abbie" Brunies were not reticent in saying "We got all that stuff from the colored musicians."[18] Paul Mares, leader of the Chicago-based band called The New Orleans Rhythm Kings has been quoted as saying "We did our best to copy the colored music we'd heard at home. We did the best we could, but naturally we couldn't play real colored style."[19]

Before the District was closed in 1917 all the early Dixielanders had been able to hear the colored bands of Storyville. By that time, in fact, there were a few white faker bands playing in the District and in other white cabarets around town. The process of change had begun.

The music of the colored bands was far too advanced for Dixielanders to imitate closely but by listening over extended periods they were able to catch phrases or choruses and gradually shape them into tunes. One of the most famous examples was Larry Sheilds' clarinet chorus of *St. Louis Blues*, originally a variation created by Louis Nelson Delisle the Creole clarinetist.[20]

These non-readers did not understand ragtime music. Most of them were blues players, they considered ragtime as a generic term for any music that was not blues or was played faster than blues. They had only the vaguest ideas about music, knowing nothing of chords, keys, harmonies, bass figures or time signatures. They were, in a word, the type of fakers known as "Routiners". This is a term meaning the band fashioned a routine, usually consisting of verse, chorus and one or two variation choruses, rehearsing this routine repeatedly until it was memorized. When playing for the public the routine of each tune was simply repeated for as long as required. Familiarity with the routine, after much repetition, made it possible to increase the tempo. From the faker's point of view it is effective to do so because mistakes can be masked, fluffs can be glossed over and music is easier to improvise—a feature not usually understood by the general public. The increased tempo had wide appeal to the post-war fad for faster dances, resulting in great popularity for the dixieland bands of the early 1920s.

The repeat of the routine was concealed on the three-minute 78 r.p.m. records of that period so the limited ability of the routiner bands has been overlooked. Once a routine is learned no further musical or artistic effort is required, the routine is simply followed in a stereotyped manner. This process is the antithesis of New Orleans music where originality is essential to create variation.

Routiner bands, as with other faker bands, need a reader or at least a speller of music to guide them in setting their routines. Eddie Edwards, the trombone player, filled that role for The Original Dixieland Jazz Band. Unfortunately for him, he could not claim any credit for the successful routines of the band because of the publicity stunts of Nick LaRocca. Although LaRocca was an inept cornetist, he was a consummate public-relations man. He proclaimed to the Press and to anyone who would listen that the success of the band was due to their inability to read music, thus managing to make a virtue of their musical illiteracy. Strangely, such nonsense is still believed in certain circles.

There is some disagreement whether the word jazz, or jass as it was then spelled, was applied to Tom Brown's band, the first dixieland band to reach Chicago or to Stein's band, the second one to arrive in that city. There is no disagreement however, that the term was coined in Chicago. Perhaps it is worth noting that this first use of the word jazz was applied by white promoters to the sounds produced by white routiners. New Orleans musicians did not use the word, always insisting they played music, not jazz. It was only after leaving New Orleans that some of the musicians accepted the term. In view of this another definition of jazz might be: "A formularized sound produced by white routiner bands that have no understanding of music." Very little improvisation was involved in the routines of these first jazz bands. If part of the routine was forgotten—not an uncommon event with fakers—something would have to be hastily improvised. Otherwise jazz initially was all very methodical.

Beginning with the dixieland bands the recording industry has had great influence on American music but recordings at first had limited effect because of the curious phenomena of race records. Recording companies presumably thought there was one kind of music fit for white people to hear and another type of music suitable only for the ears of the "Black race." Possessing little knowledge of music they made that judgment in the same way as the southern bigots, that is, by the color of the musician's skin. Recordings by white musicians were sold in white neighborhoods; those by non-white musicians were only available in Black communities. Throughout the 1920s white people were deprived of the genuine dance music of New Orleans on records. They were restricted to hearing what has been described as "rinky tink" music.

By the late 1920s the situation began to change with the release of records now called Chicago style. These were recordings made by young white men who had heard New Orleans colored bands playing on the south side of Chicago. Unlike the Dixielanders, the Chicagoans had a good understanding of music, they were reading musicians definitely not confined to the playing of simple routines. Mezz Mezzrow, one of the leading Chicagoans, in relating the circumstances of their first recording date stated the preparations included the writing of new musical introductions for the tunes. Describing these recordings Mezzrow said:

"With these records, Chicago style was defined for all time for better and for worse. A gang of myths has sprung up around them, but one thing they really prove is that we were a plenty uneven and erratic bunch of performers even at the height of our Chicago careers, and that's the truth—guys with a lot of talent, maybe, but not by a long shot a well-established and independent group. Our music was *derived*, that's what these records show; we took some things over from the colored musicians (the flare-up, the explosion, shuffle rhythm, the break) and sometimes did them good; we drifted away from their pattern in places and fell down. The Chicago school was a turning-point along the line of march, a betwixt-and-between affair; it was a halfway house . . . "[21]

But this "derived" music was played by white musicians thus demonstrating the absurdity of segregated music. Eventually race records quietly disappeared from the market.

Undeniably Chicago style was largely imitative and from that standpoint alone it did not approximate the New Orleans style. The Chicagoans were unable to fully comprehend the principles of New Orleans music but they knew it to be an original and attractive sound worthy of continuance.

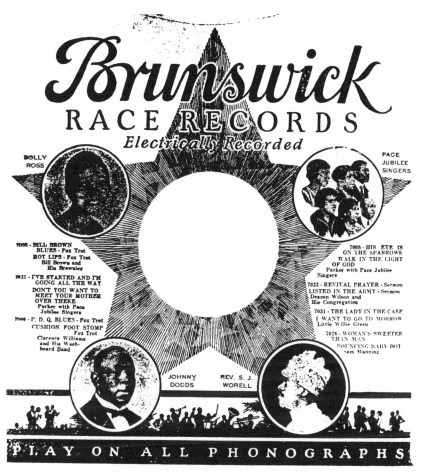

A Race Record cover of the 1920's.

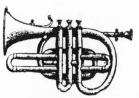

Keep this Card You May
Need It

KID ALBERT JAZZ BAND

Music Furnished For All Occasions
Tom Albert, Leader
Res 512 Dauphine St Main 4565-L

Jules Barnes, Mgr.   Res. 2610 Eight St. Uptown 4825-2411

Joe Lee, Asst. Mgr. 2217 Amelia Phone Up. 2411

New Orleans, La.

Original Maple Leaf Novelty Jazz
- - Orchestra. - -

Octave Gaspard, Mgr.   1728 Marais St.
Phone Hemlock 1035

MUSIC FURNISHED FOR ALL OCCASIONS
Always Call Hemlock 1035

Victor Gaspard, Asst. Mgr.
1525 Allen St.   Phone Hemlock 2381

Business cards from the early 1920s.

MAGNOLIA 7

John Casimir

YOUNG TUXEDO BAND

PHILIP STREET   NEW ORLEANS, LOUISIANA

P. Humphrey, Leader   **W. Pajaud, Ass't Leader**

Eureka Brass Band

Music For All Occasions

J. Clark Gen. Mgr.   New Orleans
Louisiana

Business cards from the 1950s.

Chicago style can be considered as the second offspring to issue from the music of New Orleans played this time not by fakers but by young men already proficient in music. The well-rehearsed arrangements on these records reflect the efforts made by the young Chicagoans to employ some of the techniques of New Orleans style variation. But Chicago style had a short lifetime. Its practitioners soon digressed; on the one hand to simple small band improvised jazz and on the other hand to the orchestrated style of the large swing bands.

The Chicago musicians were able to approach closer to the music of New Orleans partially because as Northerners they did not suffer from the handicap of racial prejudice to the same extent as the southern Dixielanders. Some of them even developed a sort of hero worship similar to that accorded the musicians by the populace of New Orleans. Still the Chicagoans could not overcome the mental obstruction of the improvisation concept in order to proceed to a more advanced stage.

Mezzrow, who was not familiar with New Orleans and its special social environment, described the music of a New Orleans band—which he called a jazz band—as follows:

"The jazz band was made up out of the main instruments in the street band, and they worked up ideas taken over from the blues and worksongs of the colored folks, plus the fast stepping music of the marching societies. Into their improvisation, not thinking about it, just letting all the stored-up music in their skulls percolate around some, they wove the stomps and joys and hollers, the shouts and laments, the gavottes and quadrilles, all the different kinds of music that came from the Creole string trios and Storyville whorehouse pianos, and from the levee and the riverboat and the picnic grounds and the burial grounds too . . ."[22]

Similar views have been echoed in jazz books by the score. But the Creole music of those places, as we have been able to observe, was based on orthodox principles of music—on "strictly music", in Morton's terms. Unfortunately Mezzrow could not escape from the simplistic belief that the music was somehow able to just "percolate around" in the musicians skulls and emerge as improvisation. Or in other words, as some sort of non-intellectual instinct. A posture not so very different from the attitude of the uninformed Southerners who thought it was an African instinct from the Congo jungle.

The sub-division of small band improvised jazz that arose from Chicago style is now commonly called dixieland jazz. It is not quite the same as the earlier dixieland jazz of the routiners. To be sure there is a certain routine involved, however instead of the whole band playing a tune by rote, these later day dixielanders use the improvised solo by rote.

Typically in this plan the first and last choruses are played in what is called collective improvisation, which is a euphemistic way of saying every man for himself. The intervening choruses consist of a succession of improvised solos by some or all of the instruments in the band. With this simple procedure there is no need for the rehearsals of the earlier faker bands in order to learn how to play the routine together. The grouping is not really a band at all, in the older sense of the word, it is more accurately described as an assembly of individual soloists held together by loud mechanical-sounding drum and cymbal beats. There is less need for co-operation in the band. The atmosphere becomes competitive with the result that each man plays *fortissimo*, as loud as possible. And the blatancy is compounded by the inclusion of a banjo in the rhythm section which gives a clangorous sound.

Creativity is not required in such a methodical musical setting, indeed it might prove deleterious. Simple faking or improvising is sufficient, which should not be regarded as creative even if the player has an understanding of music. Artistry is out of place here and originality a definite handicap.

With few exceptions the repertoire of these bands is confined to imitations of records made in the 1920s. Imitation may be the highest form of flattery or the lowest form of larceny depending upon the circumstances and the point of view but applied here, whatever it may be, it is not New Orleans music. The musicians of New Orleans took some pride in their originality, in not imitating the variations or arrangements of other musicians, for that reason New Orleans music was always in a state of constant development. For dixieland jazz, however, the music has remained static, rooted in the 1920s recordings of New Orleans and other bands. Because dixieland bands play more or less the same tunes in more or less the same way often there is difficulty distinguishing one band from another. At dixieland festivals groups from Japan, Europe, Australia and various parts of America including New Orleans all sound very similar. The method is so facile it has spread world wide and has become what might be called the world style dixieland jazz formula.

Despite these limitations the style has maintained a certain popularity with a portion of the public as "good time music" illustrating that even in this emasculated, diluted and deformed version New Orleans music has managed to preserve some of its charm.

CHAPTER 16

THE BIG BANDS

Unlike the earlier stages of American music the period of the big bands is well documented. With the widespread use of radio and recording in the 1930s and 1940s those bands became very popular not just with dancers but also with the general public. The prime focus here is placing the large dance bands in their historical context. Previously, with the sole exception of the New Orleans brass bands, American dance music had been provided by small units. The big bands, usually consisting of twelve to fifteen instruments, represented a significant development gradually achieved during the decade of the 1920s.

For the most part the big bands fell into three categories. The sweet bands played soothing music strictly as written. The mechanical bands played with a machine-like precision and with little latitude for variation. Most popular were the swing bands for which the period is named and which conformed with the principles of New Orleans music.

The word swing as applied to music is undoubtedly older than the style it purports to represent. Most likely it began as an adjective used in New Orleans to describe a type of dance rhythm. Perhaps the first documented use of the word as applied to music occurred on February 18, 1924 when the New Orleans Creole orchestra of Armand J. Piron recorded a tune entitled *Louisiana Swing*.

Sometimes swing music is perceived as the second sub-division of Chicago style because a number of the Chicagoans achieved success in the milieu. In reality Chicago style had a relatively small impact upon swing music although some famous swing musicians began their careers in Chicago or were influenced by the Chicago style.

To make the music have a swing beat the best of the big

bands consisted of highly competent musicians playing well thought-out orchestrations to which they were able to add, subtract or variate. They were capable of playing all kinds of music in a swinging manner as previously the New Orleans bands had played music for all occasions in the New Orleans style.

The origin of the swing band can be traced back to the early tin bands of New Orleans. We have seen how the tin band was formed from the admixture of brass, string and woodwind instruments. With the later addition of the bass fiddle and especially the drum set—that is, the snare drum combined with the bass drum operated by a foot pedal—these amalgamated groups began calling themselves orchestras. In a similar manner as the array of instruments in the brass bands which could be changed, augmented or decreased as the occasion demanded, so this basic arrangement of instruments in the dance orchestra was flexible and capable of enlargement or reduction.

A photograph of the John Robichaux orchestra probably dating from the late 1890s reveals how the small tin band had grown into an eight-piece orchestra. Depicted in the band are two violins from the string band, a trombone and two cornets (E flat and B flat) from the brass band plus a bass fiddle, clarinet and a very early model of a combined snare and bass drum set.[23]

Robichaux was originally from Thibodaux, Louisiana. He was not, in New Orleans terms, a musicianer. Although a reader he was considered an inferior violinist who played in a left-handed position. In the photo, seated at the center, he has posed with the violin held in the conventional (or customary) manner but has neglected to change the position of his bow and the chin rest. There are other interesting features shown in this 19th century photograph. Chandler's homemade foot pedal can be seen positioned on the bass drum, when the pedal was depressed the drum and side cymbal were struck simultaneously. Other drum set equipment such as a stand for the snare drum had yet to be invented so Chandler hung the snare drum from the side of the bass drum. The wire hook for that purpose is visible on the snare drum.

New Orleans string band musicians traditionally were seated but brass band musicians played in a standing position.

The John Robichaux Orchestra of the late 1890's. Standing, left to right, are Baptiste Delisle, James Wilson (E flat cornet), James Macneil, Octave Gaspard. Seated, left to right, are Didi Chandler (note homemade bass drum foot pedal), Charles McCurdy (with three clarinets), John Robichaux, Wendell Macneil.

The Superior Orchestra 1908. Left to right are Walter Brundy, Buddy Johnson, Bunk Johnson, Peter Bocage, Louis Nelson Delisle, Richard Payne, Billy Marrero.

The Imperial Orchestra 1908. Left to right are John MacMurray, George Filhe, Jimmy Palao, Louis Nelson Delisle, Rene Baptiste, Manuel Perez, James Brown.

The first mixed instrument tin bands did not change that custom; brass players standing behind the seated stringed instruments. With the addition of the drums played in a seated position and the bass viol played in a standing posture that arrangement began to change.

Another tradition portrayed is the position of the string bass at the left of the band and the drums and trombone on the right. The Robichaux band did not have a guitar player, normally positioned next to the bass viol. The guitarist's place was taken by Wendell Macneil, a highly respected musician who played violin with the band for many years, bolstering the weak playing of Robichaux. Macneil may have been the real music leader of the orchestra.

Photographs of the Imperial and Superior orchestras taken about the year 1908 show how a seven-piece band had become the standard with two brass and three stringed instruments plus the clarinet and drums.[24]

A few years later the white routiner dixieland bands were formed with only five instruments, accomplished by omitting the violin and substituting the piano for the bass and guitar. Probably the piano substitution was an idea first suggested to the young Dixielanders from observing Manetta's Tuxedo band playing in the District. The incentive for smaller units was the advantage to be gained over other bands by being able to charge less money for playing an engagement. Not bound by the ancient traditions of the colored bands the Dixielanders were able to benefit from the five-piece groups which could be hired at a lower cost.

These small bands began to take a sizable amount of work away from the larger seven piece colored bands so it became necessary to meet the competition by reducing still further the number of men in the band. For the first time in the long history of New Orleans dance music the violin began to be omitted from some of the dance bands, partly in response to the competition and partly because the ancient tradition of the string band had faded into the past.

The loss of the violin left a six-piece band of three rhythm instruments and the cornet, clarinet and trombone. The typical arrangement of what is now called a classic or traditional jazz

250

band. Many older musicians regretted losing the violin from the New Orleans dance bands, saying it changed the nature of the variations and allowed the volume of sound to increase to a level of blatancy, impeding the dynamics of the orchestra.

At this point then, about the time of the first World War, the development of the dance bands had progressed from the primary amalgamation of the tin band through the orchestra stage and on into the six-piece so-called traditional jazz band.

When saxophones became available another and far reaching period of development began in the instrumentation of dance bands. The gradual addition of saxophones restricted stringed instruments to a rhythm section of guitar, bass fiddle, piano and drums so that the big bands became an amalgam of brass, reed and rhythm sections—the culmination of fifty years of development from the original tin bands. Saxophones were an important part of this combination, impelling a smoother rhythm. The peculiar aspect of the saxophone allows for a more fluid blending of notes. Several of them, acting as a section, are an essential element in causing the music to 'swing'.

Initially the saxophone was regarded as a freak. A hybrid conical brass instrument with keys resembling a clarinet and possessing a woodwind mouthpiece. Soon it became apparent that this freakish instrument was easy to play, much easier than the clarinet. Clarinet players had no difficulty in doubling on the saxophone, those unable to master the clarinet could still play the saxophone with ease.

By the early 1920s saxophones appeared in many dance bands increasing the volume of sound to justify the use of the banjo and bass horn. Later this music was to be called New Orleans jazz but the musicians continued to think of themselves as musicians playing music not jazzmen playing jazz.

By coincidence this was the time when non-white bands began to make recordings. In 1923 Joe "King" Oliver's Creole Jazz Band with a rhythm section of piano, banjo and drums used a C-Melody saxophone on one set of recordings and a bass saxophone on another recording date. Also in 1923 A. J. Piron's Orchestra began a series of recordings using a bass horn and two saxophones. This band, composed largely of Creole musicians, had the three section format of the later swing bands with two brass and two reeds plus the four rhythm instruments that became the standard number in swing band rhythm sections. It was an early example of a swing-type transition band which would lead to the larger groups of the 1930s.

By 1926, under the name of The Dixie Syncopaters, Joe Oliver was employing sections of three brass and three reeds and had adopted the four-piece rhythm section. And in 1930 the orchestra had progressed to a big band of five brass, four reed and four rhythm instruments, omitting the banjo to return to the guitar, and serving as a typical example of how the big bands developed.

The New Orleans Creole bands were recorded on race records not sold to the white public, but that was no deterrent to the young aspiring white musicians around Chicago who eagerly purchased race records on the South Side of the city where they were readily available. Mezz Mezzrow has described how the youngsters learned about New Orleans music from listening to the records made by the New Orleans musicians:

"Night after night as soon as we finished work at White City we'd shoot over to my house for a record-playing session... I was beginning to collect hot records like some guys collect telephone numbers, and the ones I had would make a record-fan's head spin around like a turntable... We were always jumping up and putting the needle back to play a good passage over." [25]

The Chicagoans were not the only musicians listening intently to the recordings of the New Orleans bands, other musicians began to grasp some of the rudiments of New Orleans dance music. It was in these dance bands of the 1920s that many musicians served a sort of apprenticeship.

As the New Orleans style of dance music spread it caught the attraction of the public. Dancing became a fad of the 1920s "jazz age" just as it had in New Orleans during the eighteenth and nineteenth centuries. Ever larger dance halls and dance palaces were built to accommodate the crowds of people who wished to dance to this 'new' and exciting style of music. As the size of the dance halls grew so did the size of the bands in order to fill the acoustic requirements of the cavernous buildings not then fitted with microphones and broadcasting equipment.

252

With the larger bands more emphasis was placed upon written orchestrations. The big bands were not the place for fakers; the men had to be good reading musicians able to play the arrangements as written. This, again, was in accordance with New Orleans dance bands which also used arrangements, even including drum charts, illustrated by drummer Warren "Baby" Dodds' account of his experience, in 1921, on first joining Joe Oliver's band in California:

"...When I got there the first piece of music they put in front of me was *Canadian Capers*. I asked Joe how he was going to play it. He said from the left hand corner to the right hand corner; from top to bottom. The trio was in the middle of the number. I said 'Kick off', and Joe kicked off. I read that piece of music down, from side to side and went back to the trio. I had played that number once and I knew it, so I began playing my own style of drums..."[26]

Some of the Chicago youngsters realized the New Orleans bands used arrangements. In Benny Goodman's book *The Kingdom Of Swing,* Gil Rodin, a member of the Ben Pollack Band and later a leading light of the Bob Crosby co-operative band is cited:

"There were such places as the Lincoln Gardens, a vast barn of a structure at 31st and Gordon, where Armstrong made his first appearance (in 1922) in the orchestra of King Oliver, with the Dodds brothers, and Bill Johnson (bass). It was here according to Gil Rodin, that a musician could hear a band play *arranged* music and still keep swinging—something that did not make its appearance in the general current of jazz music until nearly a decade later."[27]

Viewed from the bandstand, so to speak, Baby Dodds commented on the Oliver band in Chicago:

"In 1922 King Oliver took his band to Chicago where we played in the Lincoln Gardens...It was merely a hall with benches placed around for people to sit on...One couldn't help but dance to that band...It was a dance band that liked to play anything...We worked to make music, and we played music to make people like it. The Oliver band played for the comfort of the people. Not so they couldn't hear, or so they had to put their fingers in their ears, nothing like that. Sometimes the band played so softly you could hardly hear it, but still you knew the music was going. We played so soft that you could often hear the people's feet dancing. The music was so soothing and then when we put a little jump into it the patrons just had to dance . . . And when we worked a number out and rehearsed it we always played it that way . . .

The Oliver Band was traditional and Joe was always doing things according to the New Orleans tradition. Sometimes when the band started a number there would be one beat on the bass drum, or the piano would have a couple of notes to pick up, or even Joe on the cornet. But it wasn't more than a couple of notes. It is New Orleans tradition that when there is an introduction everybody hits that introduction. The whole band had to start together and finish together. No sloppy start or ending was permitted. We did these things correctly and that is why our band sounded so good.

Even the lineup on the bandstand was in New Orleans tradition. From our left to right there was the bass, then the piano, then the clarinet, next to the clarinet was Louis on second trumpet and Joe was next to him. Next to Joe was Dutrey on trombone, and my drums were next to the trombone. The banjo was next to the piano but either a little in back or in front of the piano, next to the treble keys. The lineup at the Lincoln Gardens bandstand was arranged in such a way as to make the music sound better. In other words, it gave good balance and improved the sound . . .

Not all the people came to the Lincoln Gardens to dance. Some of the white musicians came to hear our band, Benny Goodman, Jess Stacey, Frank Teschmacher, Dave Tough, Bud Freeman and Ben Pollack used to come to listen . . ."[28]

Here we see the process of learning by listening, used in the District by the youthful future dixieland routiners, repeated in Chicago a decade or so later by the youthful future swing musicians.

It is interesting to note how Oliver adhered to the tradition of New Orleans music, using the straight line arrangement of the band first devised on the balconies of the New Orleans dance halls. The lead instruments were in the center with the harmony and rhythm instruments at the ends of the lineup. In

Chicago the band dispensed with the violin lead it had previously used on the west coast in 1921 with Jimmy Palao. Instead Oliver brought his protege Louis Armstrong into the band, but the Oliver Band was still able to make use of dynamic variation, playing very softly at times.[29]

Relevant also is Dodds' remark about rehearsals. In the same way as the earlier Creole bands and the later swing bands, Oliver's band always played a tune the way it had been rehearsed. So much for the role of improvisation in the King Oliver band and, we may safely infer from this evidence alone since Oliver was a stickler for Creole tradition, for all New Orleans Creole bands.[30]

Dodds tells us the Oliver Band, again in the typical manner of Creole bands, "liked to play anything". That is to say all kinds of music, or music for all occasions. But as he makes clear, only Oliver and Dutrey were Creoles able to speak the Creole-French language. In a San Francisco dance hall the band was accused of being "niggers" not Creoles. Oliver and Dutrey began speaking Creole and so avoided a racial incident.[31]

Dodds seems to suggest this was a ruse of the San Francisco local union to put the New Orleans competition out of business. From our point of view it is apropos to see how, even as late as the 1920s, the Creole language could still be employed as a defensive expedient as it had been used during the time of slavery.

Increasingly, the technique of arranging music for large bands became more specialized. Arrangers for colored bands, in particular, became very skillful in their ability to exploit the sections of the orchestra. For example, the bands of Doc Cook, Benny Moten, Jelly Roll Morton, Luis Russell, and the "Royal Creolians" of Walter Barnes, tragically fated to perish in a dance hall fire, had groups varying in size from ten to fourteen pieces during the 1920s. These bands and others featured arrangements some of which are still considered classics of their kind. In the course of that decade the dance music of New Orleans was gradually transformed, modified and to an extent simplified to suit the requirements of the larger bands.

And this was the third offshoot of the New Orleans style.

There is an impression that swing music began with the

success of the Benny Goodman Orchestra in 1935. In reality big band swing music was in a continuous state of development throughout the 1920s. The Fletcher Henderson Band with arrangers such as Don Redman and Benny Carter earned a reputation for adept orchestrations. By the early 1930s the Henderson band had grown to include five brass instruments consisting of three trumpets and two trombones, a four man reed section of clarinet and saxophone players, and a rhythm section of piano, guitar, string bass and drums.

Following Henderson's example, Benny Goodman formed a similar thirteen-piece band plus himself as the featured clarinetist. Goodman purchased a number of superior orchestrations from Henderson and other colored arrangers and band leaders. Some of the arrangements were written as much as ten years earlier and had been previously recorded by colored bands. As those were issued on race records, however, they were completely unknown to white audiences and became big hits for the Goodman band.

The newly developed phenomena of radio broadcasting had a powerful influence in popularizing swing music imparting an aura of dignity not formerly enjoyed. Some of the nation-wide weekly radio shows, with audiences numbering in the millions, featured the music of the large bands. The repeal of the prohibition laws enabled the lowly illegal speakeasy to become transformed into the elegant and fashionable night club offering swing dance music for their patron's enjoyment. And large hotels were able to expand their ballroom activities often including live late-night broadcasts directly from the hotel bandstands. Due to the regional time difference those dance music broadcasts were heard on the west coast during the early evening hours reaching a much wider audience than in the eastern States where they originated. When the Goodman band played in Los Angeles in 1935 it was already well known from these broadcasts, surprising everyone by playing to sell-out crowds at the Palomar Ballroom.

A further impetus contributing to the success of the Goodman band and other swing bands was the continuing improvement in the quality of electrical recordings, allowing a better appreciation of the swing sound. No longer derided as "nigger

The fourteen piece big band of Benny Goodman in 1936. (l. to r.) Rhythm section: Jess Stacey, piano; Harry Goodman, bass; Allen Reuss, guitar; Gene Krupa, drums. Brass section: Harry Geller, Ralph Muzillo, Nate Kazebier, trumpets; Joe Harris, Red Ballard, trombones. Reed section: Dick Clark, Bill Depew, Hymie Schertzer, Art Rollini. Standing: Helen Ward, vocalist, and Benny Goodman.

music" although ironically often featuring tunes and arrangements by colored musicians, this third derivation of the New Orleans style—swing music—became respectable to the enthusiastic general public. A high point of respectability was reached with the 1938 Carnegie Hall concerts of the Goodman Orchestra.

Band leaders were careful to encourage this air of esteem by furnishing decorative music stands, neat uniforms for the men and often having a girl singer, impeccably groomed, gowned and coiffured, sit in front of the band. Discipline in the swing bands became formidable, some leaders instituting a system of fines for minor infractions. The 1930s being depression years when high paying jobs or work of any kind was hard to find, it was not too difficult to enforce the rules of conduct and to ensure the orchestrations were played as written.

During the 1920s musicians of both races had occasionally played together in private sessions and on recordings. By the late 1930s as swing music gained respectability it became possible, for the first time, to gradually begin the process of integrating the musicians in public. After almost two hundred years of development this was an immense and revolutionary step forward in the history of American music. Benny Goodman especially deserves recognition for his contribution to the public integration of the swing bands.[32]

The basic ingredients of swing music were derived from the New Orleans style but stress was laid on just a few of the simpler effects such as the solo and the repeated figure—called a "riff" because it was sometimes indicated on music scores by the letters "R.F." Although many of the orchestrations were ingenuous compared to what was being done a decade earlier, it still required skilled musicianship and disciplined teamwork to make the music "swing." These are qualities very much respected by New Orleans musicians. Discipline in the swing bands, however, was imposed by the leader whereas in New Orleans music the discipline was expected to be self-imposed.

In retrospect it seems leader-imposed discipline was entirely necessary for the swing bands were composed of musicians from different musical environments with divergent musical ideas. On the other hand New Orleans musicians were from a single musical background. They had similar aims and ideas about what they were trying to accomplish, not needing an imposed discipline to strive for what they considered to be good music. Parenthetically it can be noted that in the post-swing era when musicians played improvisational jazz without orderly restraints the resulting sounds were tolerable only to the tone-deaf and were strong arguments for the return of discipline in music.

In the music of the big bands the main emphasis was placed upon section playing and for this purpose rehearsals were of great importance. Some leaders encouraged the brass or reed sections to rehearse their parts separately. Advising leaders of swing bands, Goodman wrote:

"If you're working with a bigger band—anything from nine or ten up to fourteen—it might be a good idea for the reeds and brass to go off separately before or after the main rehearsal, and work on things by themselves. These are what we call section rehearsals, and even in big bands, like mine or Dorsey's or almost any one you can mention, you'll frequently find the four fellows in the sax section, or the three trumpets getting off by themselves to straighten out some quartet or trio in an arrangement, or work up a figure to fit in a spot."[33]

New Orleans musicians also used this method of rehearsal. Speaking of Luis Russell's 1929 band, for example, the bass player Pops Foster said:

"Russell's band was romping so good in '29 we had everything sewed up around New York. We were playing the same style we played back in New Orleans.

Some of the guys in New York used to call us the rehearsal band because we rehearsed a lot. But you've got to rehearse to get things together no matter what kind of band you've got. We used to have separate rehearsals for the saxes, the trumpets, the bass, the reeds and the rhythm. I had to make them all to pick out the rhythm. By the time we played a show, I knew the music so good I never looked at it. Even when you rehearse, you've still got to play with the guys for a while before you know what they're going to do. A lot of the bands were just screaming bands; they're not really doing nothing but screaming. Most of the white bands think if you're not blowing loud you're not playing nothing. None of them want to study tonation, they just want to blow."[34]

Foster's remarks about screaming and insistence upon "tonation" should be noted. Playing within the normal range of the instrument and a good tone are essential ingredients of New Orleans music.

Jazz critics and the jazz fraternity in general derided swing music for its strict adherence to written scores, claiming there was nothing original in the music of the big bands. A view not shared by New Orleans musicians who greatly admired the sounds of swing, recognizing the amount of rehearsal and the high degree of skill required to produce those sounds.

With the larger number of instruments in a swing band the possibilities for variation can be increased by using sections of the orchestra as separate groups. Orchestral or sectional variation was a feature of the brass bands but it had not been utilized to any great extent in the tin bands, the string bands, or the small dance orchestras of New Orleans. In those small groups there were no recognizable sections; they operated as integral units, all the instruments continuing to play throughout the duration of the tune. The sectional arranging of swing music, therefore, opened a field of dance music variation previously not fully explored. Nevertheless, it was precisely within the tradition of New Orleans music in that it provided another way for variation to be brought to dance music and it allowed for fuller chordal tone patterns to further beautify the music.

It is true these were scored variations but New Orleans musicians do not draw a distinction between written variations and those played extempore. That is a trite disparity made by naive "jazzologists" and devotees of improvisation. The requirement for variation is that it should enhance the beauty of the music regardless of its spontaneity. Arrangers who take the time to work out attractive variations can bring pleasing and memorable qualities to music and of course written variation can also be subject to extempore variation should the occasion arise.

In this respect the sections of the big bands could be managed in several ways. For example arrangers could alternate one section for melody and another for harmony or have the melody played against a riff-based harmonic background. With the interspersion of solos this method could bring variation to the orchestra without necessarily varying the melody. That is to say melodic variation could be augmented or supplanted by instrumental or orchestral variation.

Some of the most successful arrangements of this type were those of the Artie Shaw band of 1938-1939. Shaw has described how he studied the hit records made by other bands to discover ways to emulate their success:

"The thing that each of these hit records had, it seemed to me, was a crystal-clear transparency. Not only in the recording, but in the arranging as well. You could hear every single last instrument on the record. The arrangement itself was simple, essentially, as a result even a lay listener could (so to speak) see all the way through the surface of the music right down to the bottom, as when you look into a clear pool of water and see the sound at the very bottom of the pool.

That was the image that occurred to me. And from there on in, that was what I tried to get my arrangements to sound like, whether I made it myself or not. And if anyone brought in an arrangement which fell short of this criterion I had established for myself—that arrangement was out.

All this took a long time. Not only the arranging but the development of a blend between the various sections of the band as well as the blend in the sections themselves—but by the time the whole thing was finished, the musical job was done."[35]

This fifteen-piece band achieved a blend of instrumental sound to some degree comparable with the great Creole brass bands. It consisted of three trumpets, three trombones, five reeds and the usual four rhythm instruments of piano, guitar, string bass and drums. By judicious use of the trombones another section, in effect, was brought into the orchestrations. The members of the band, for the most part, were young men with little prior experience as professional musicians since, as Shaw stated, at that time he could not afford to pay the higher salaries of more experienced men. The emphasis of the orchestrations therefore was heavily placed upon the sections, with comparatively few intricate melodic variations and those played mostly by Shaw as clarinet solos.

Shaw implies these were relatively straightforward arrangements pointing up an important principle long known to New Orleans musicians but not generally understood—that the complexity or simplicity of music has little direct relationship to the intrinsic beauty of sound. When an attractive melody is well rehearsed and well executed with correct harmony and good rhythm it has small need of further embellishment. Among the recorded examples of this type of orchestration during the band's brief existence were the hit tune *Begin The Beguine, Softly As In A Morning Sunrise* and the hauntingly beautiful *Yesterdays*. In 1938 and 1939 the band was proclaimed for 'making dance history' because, as earlier in New Orleans, people found it delightful to dance to such music.

The Shaw band also gave a demonstration of how the repeated figure or riff could be used as a thematic variation with the arrangement of the tune *Oh Lady Be Good* which, it will be remembered, was used as a march by the New Orleans brass bands. On this 1939 recording, after the opening chorus stating the theme, the succeeding choruses consist of riffs, each chorus a different riff variant. In addition, during the last chorus there was a fine example of the abrupt, sharply defined open breaks typical of this band, good swing music, and the New Orleans style. Here we see how the element of musical surprise so much appreciated by New Orleans musicians can be used even in a swing band arrangement comprised mainly of riffs. This record is a primer for those seeking to understand how, by imaginative arranging, the repeated figure can be employed as a swing band variation, not merely a monotonous repetition of a musical phrase.

Before the invention of amplified electrical instruments dance hall entrepreneurs preferred loud dance bands to attract crowds of people. Shaw noted the loudness of this band—a common complaint with reed instrument players. On the bandstands built for the big bands often the reeds were seated directly in front of the brass section. However, the volume of sound did allow dynamic variation previously unattainable with small bands and in later years Shaw, a severe critic, recognized the "remarkable intensity" of the band.

Shaw selected tunes written by successful composers of

popular music, tunes with pleasing melodic qualities, concentrating upon playing them correctly, with discipline, and without becoming too ornate. By so doing this band achieved a high percentage of artistically first-class recordings many of which are regarded as swing classics and were admired by New Orleans musicians.[36]

Several swing bands of the 1920s and 1930s contained small groups—a band within the band—that played small band swing music. An early example, in the mid-1920s, was the group named Cookie's Gingersnaps, part of the Charles "Doc" Cook Orchestra. Ultimately, that led to Jimmie Noone's Apex Club Orchestra, sometimes cited as the first small swing band to appear on records. As a New Orleans musician, it is apparent that Noone intended his band to parallel the early tin bands. The lead role formerly assigned to the violin was replaced by the alto saxophone allowing the clarinet to play counterpoint and second part harmony variations as it had done in the tin bands. The recordings by Noone's small band give us an idea of how those early tin bands sounded and in the way they operated.

Another interesting small group was the Clambake Seven contingent of Tommy Dorsey's band. Between 1935 and 1939 the Dorsey band, in both the large and small versions, recorded swing music played in a manner conforming to the standards and principles of New Orleans music. Their 1936 recording of *Maple Leaf Rag* is an example of how ragtime could be readily incorporated into swing music as previously it had been assimilated by the New Orleans bands. Ragtime tunes were usually too protracted to conform with the three minute 78 r.p.m. records of the period, consequently they were either abbreviated or recorded *allegro,* as in this instance.

The 1930s co-operative big band fronted by the singer Bob Crosby and its small group called The Bobcats contained several skilled New Orleans white musicians of a later generation than the dixieland routiners. The arrangements of this band reflected the dixieland sound in an improved, more musical mode. One of their most successful recordings entitled *South Rampart Street Parade* gave evidence in the title and orchestration of how those young musicians had learned from the New Orleans brass bands. Until the late 1950s, when the character of the neighborhood began to change, South Rampart Street was a route frequently used by the parades of the colored societies in New Orleans.[37]

The big swing bands occasionally adapted classical music for the dance, a process called swinging the classics, thus following the example set by the New Orleans musicians of the 19th. century. Again demonstrating how the principles of swing music were closely related to those of New Orleans music. Both styles could be adapted to any kind of music.

The sectional orchestrations of the big bands was the last significant development in the New Orleans style of dance music. After the late 1940s the functional role of music declined as the dancing of embraced couples became less popular. The smaller groups that replaced the big dance bands were directed at entertainment for passive audiences, they did not utilize the principles of music discussed here and are outside the scope of this history.

Viewed in retrospect it seems a music designed to accompany neighborhood parades, dances and community affairs will not thrive when it is divorced from those surroundings and activities. Historically, it has always been true that when a social environment undergoes change its culture, including its music, has also had to change and adapt. Swing music and dixieland jazz emerged from the music of New Orleans but until a demand for such locally supported functional music should return the parental style appears to have run its course. This is a natural phenomena disturbing only if the music form should be allowed to expire without its aims, accomplishments and true historical record being recognized.

Notes for Part IV

1. James Parton, *General Butler in New Orleans* (New York: Mason Bros. 1864). Six days earlier, on May 9, 1862, the *Daily Picayune* under Union control had also commented on the "shameless conduct" of some New Orleans women and had demanded their arrest "whether arrayed in fine clothes or not."

2. The report was not forgotten by the Creoles. It was mentioned by Desdunes in *Nos Hommes et Notre Histoire.*

3. A failure to understand that pimps are always in control of the financial affairs of prostitution can lead to error. There has been a story of the pimp George Kilshaw absconding with "Lulu White's money" in 1907. As Kilshaw was Lulu White's pimp that would be tantamount to stealing his own money. The fact is Kilshaw remained in charge of Mahogany Hall brothel until the closing of the District.

4. Lulu White was famous for her diamonds. Any money she was permitted to retain probably would have been invested in this way.

5. Morton, *Library of Congress recordings,* 1938. Pianists in the District usually acquired nicknames. Manetta was known as Horse in recognition of his stamina. Morton was called Wining (Wine-ing) Boy, a reference to the champagne available in the larger brothels. Another pianist was nicknamed The Champagne Kid. According to Manetta, Morton was still a faker or poor speller at this time, not sufficiently skilled to hold a steady job but able to substitute. Manetta told how he helped with Morton's first composition *The Wining Boy Blues*, and could imitate Morton's voice soliciting for a night's work, saying "Give me a play, Horse, give me a play."

6. The rènowned pianist Wally Rose has been quoted as saying: "... Let me tell you in answer to those who think playing ragtime is easy—look at the music and you'll see it needs a hell of a lot of technique to be played well". Nat Shapiro and Nat Hentoff, eds. *Hear Me Talkin' To Ya,* (New York: Holt, Rinehart and Winston, 1955. Dover edition, 1966) p. 405.

7. The Magazine *Clef* of June 1946 contained an article by Nesuhi Ertegun entitled *Clarinet a la Creole* reporting an interview with the famous New Orleans clarinetist Albert Nicholas. It said in part: "... Nicholas has always resented the attacks of misinformed or ignorant critics on New Orleans music and musicians. To call their playing crude or primitive is, in his opinion absurd and ridiculous. The greatest among the New Orleans musicians were highly skilled and technically most proficient. Their knowledge of music went much deeper than that of most jazz celebrities of today. Manuel Perez, Peter Bocage, the Tio's, Andrew Kimball, Arnold Metoyer, Vic Gasparre, A. J. Piron and Manuel Manetta (one of the greatest musicians of all time) were a few examples he mentioned when asked to name the outstanding figures of New Orleans music."

8. *The Daily Picayune* of March 25, 1913 reported a guitar in the Tuxedo band, probably a visiting Creole musician sitting in with the band. The paper

said the band "generally constitute several brass pieces, a violin, guitar, piccolo and a piano."

9. There were four Dutrey brothers: Sam, Pete (violin), Jim (drums) and Honore.

10. Armstrong's version of this incident is given in: Louis Armstrong, *Satchmo, My life in New Orleans* (New York: Prentice-Hall, 1954).

11. Celestin's band made several recordings in the 1920s. The first session in 1925 had 'Kid Shots' Madison, cornet, and Manetta, piano. For many years Richard 'Reecarre' Alexis played cornet with the Celestin band.

12. Some of the animal sounds created as humorous effects by New Orleans musicians were later imitated by the Dixielanders, notably by the Original Dixieland Jazz Band in their recording of *Livery Stable Blues*.

13. An exception, of course, were the early French colonial musicians which had accompanied Governor De Vandreuil.

14. The working hours of slavery were noted in 1926 by Richard M. Jones with his recording of *Kin to Kant Blues*.

15. Jack Laine in conversation with the author.

16. This tune was well known to all the early Dixielanders. It was popularized as *Tiger Rag* on a 1917 recording by the Original Dixieland Jazz Band. In 1924 it was recorded in New Orleans as *Number Two Blues* by the Johnny De Droit Band although it had no relation to either ragtime or blues. Morton identified it as part of a 19th century Creole/French quadrille.

17. An unintentionally humorous book concerning the alleged origin of dixieland jazz, based largely upon interviews with LaRocca, commended the supposed merits of musical illiteracy. In a typical feat of obfuscation it contained no mention of routines, the District, or the colored musicians of New Orleans.—H.O. Brunn, *The Story of the Original Dixieland Jazz Band* (Baton Rouge: L. S. U. Press, 1960).

18. Tom Brown and Albert 'Abbie' Brunies in conversation with the author.

19. *Hear Me Talkin' To Ya*, p. 125.

20. As recalled by Professor Manetta. After the variation became popular Manetta wrote it down for his clarinet students, using it as a clarinet exercise.

21. Milton 'Mezz' Mezzrow and Bernard Wolfe, *Really The Blues* (New York: Random House, 1946), p. 156.

22. *Really The Blues*, p. 339,

23. Because of the inadequate key systems of 19th. century clarinets four types were then commonly in use: E flat, usually with brass bands; C, A, and B flat with dance bands.

24. Previously these photographs were dated five years apart, 1905 and 1910. The identical background makes that separation of dates unlikely. Professor Manetta considered both photos to have been taken in 1908, possibly on the same day.

25. *Really The Blues*. p. 116.

26. Warren 'Baby' Dodds as told to Larry Gara, *The Baby Dodds Story*. (Los Angeles: Contemporary Press, 1959.) p. 33.

27. Benny Goodman and Irving Kolodin, *The Kingdom of Swing* (New York: Stackpole, 1939. F. Ungar edition, 1961) Emphasis in original.

28. *The Baby Dodds Story*. pp. 35–37.

29. Mrs. Stella Oliver was very fond of the young Louis Armstrong. She informed the author that she had persuaded her husband, Joe, to send for Armstrong. Louis stayed at the Oliver's home in Chicago almost as an adopted son for some time after he left New Orleans. This was the reason Oliver's Chicago band had two trumpets instead of the traditional violin lead used earlier in San Francisco. Mrs. Oliver was aware, and found it amusing, that her maternal feelings were responsible for having some influence on music history.

30. An interesting comparison is Oliver's arrangement on the 1923 recording of *Dippermouth Blues* with a seven-piece band, and his recording three years later of the same tune, re-named *Sugar Foot Stomp*, with a ten-piece band. It will be noted on the later recording Oliver modified the arrangement to bring a section of three reed instruments into operation although the basic orchestration remained essentially similar.

31. *The Baby Dodds Story*. p. 34.

32. As late as the 1950s, in New Orleans, musicians were still being arrested and fined for playing in integrated bands.

33. *The Kingdom of Swing*. p. 256.

34. Pops Foster and Tom Stoddard, *Pops Foster, The Autobiography of a New Orleans Jazzman*. (Berkeley: U. C. Press, 1971) p. 159.

35. Artie Shaw, *The Trouble with Cinderella*. (New York: Farrar, Straus and Young, 1952) p. 331.
In his book Shaw remarked on "high note players" and on the ability to read music a bar ahead of the measure being played. He also emphasized the importance of rehearsals, describing a typical rehearsal session of a 1930s swing band.

36. Effective meter and tempo variations were utilized by this band. An example was the popular tune *Shine On Harvest Moon*, arranged in a manner that would have been recognized by Morton as a "stomp."

37. The title of another tune recorded by the Crosby band *Smoky Mary* was taken from the nickname of the train that ran between New Orleans and Milneburg.

SUMMARY

The history of American music reaches back much further into the past than was formerly realized. It was not invented by certain individuals or bands. It did not evolve from church music, ragtime or blues. Nor was it brought to America by slaves from Africa, although that social Darwinist theory has had great appeal. In reality it originated quite soon after New Orleans was founded and its development was proceeding long before the founding of the United States.

When much of North America was still wilderness a pocket of European, or more precisely French culture, rudely patterned after the Court of Versailles, thrived in the colonial settlement of New Orleans. Because of the isolation of that location and the surrounding physical and social environment, the culture and the music of New Orleans developed in a dramatically different way from either the European or the Anglo-American manner although it contained elements of both continents.

The French colonial system of society delegated the work of skilled labor to those colored people, usually of mixed racial ancestry, who had been declared free. These *Gens de Couleur Libres* took pride in their position as the artisans of the colonial society producing highly skilled workers of all trades including that of musician. As free and independent craftsmen not closely supervised or oppressed by colonial law they were able to develop their music in ways suitable for the special New Orleans social environment without the constraints of conventional societies.

These Creole musicians did not distinguish between various types of music. They were able to play and often compose music suitable for all manner of social occasions. The principles upon which their music was based were flexible, able to adapt to any event in the human experience from birth to death. The social activities of colonial New Orleans closely paralleled those of France, centered on the dance or *balle*. Dancing became extremely popular encouraged by the excellent music provided by the New Orleans musicians so that for many decades the city was named the Paris of America.

The invention of the steamboat and the settling of the southern States after the Louisiana Purchase enabled New Orleans to become less estranged from the rest of the continent. However, the American system of commercialized slavery brought a social environment incompatible with the more relaxed pace of French and Spanish colonialism. New Orleans became a city consisting of the new uptown American business section and the older French downtown area. They were divided by Canal Street, the widest street in America, which not only separated geographical sites but also marked the boundary between two different philosophical concepts of social behavior.

American slavery brought a further condition of seclusion to the colored Creoles. The Free Persons of Color were not permitted to assimilate into the general population as did their relatives, the white Creoles. Neither slaves nor totally free, they were placed in an anomalous position. Not accepted into the white populace and governed by special laws designed for the purpose of ultimately banning them from the state or forcing them into slavery. As a consequence the Creoles were coerced into a situation of semi-ostracism. In this seclusion their culture and their music continued to develop in unique ways throughout the period of American slavery. Tangible evidence of that musical development was shown in the design of their dance halls, especially in the types of bandstands constructed at various periods during that troubled time.

With the advent of improved brass instruments in the first half of the nineteenth century another avenue of earning a living from music opened for the creative talents of the Creole musicians. It was not unusual for some of them to play both string and brass instruments. For several decades the traditional string dance bands co-existed peacefully along with the brass bands used for parades, funerals, and various outdoor events. Sometimes those events involved dancing, but the New Orleans brass band musicians were competant to fill that need because many of them were also dance band musicians. It was thus demonstrated that people could dance to brass band music—New Orleans style—which included the use of drums. In the course of time brass bands played regularly in several dance halls of the city.

As nineteenth century New Orleans brass bands were too large for some of the smaller neighborhood dance halls the musicians ultimately contrived a smaller band which included brass, string and the newly improved woodwind instruments, particularly the clarinet. Nicknamed a tin band to distinguish it from the string and brass bands, this compromise band was the forerunner of all modern dance bands, whether of the jazz or swing variety.

During the last quarter of the nineteenth century, experimenting further with the tin band, New Orleans musicians eliminated some of the stringed instruments such as the viola and mandolin and brought the bass fiddle into the band. It was not until the late 1890s that a way was discovered for one man to play both bass and snare drums simultaneously by the use of a foot pedal fastened to the bass drum. This array of instruments was the standard New Orleans dance orchestra of the early twentieth century. Later, with the loss of the violin due to the competition of the dixieland bands, the instrumentation of the tin band was transformed into what is now known as a traditional jazz band.

During the Reconstruction years after the Civil War the Creoles struggled to achieve equality for all colored people through civil rights legislation. Eventually defeated in that purpose by the southern segregationist administrations, the Creoles gradually merged with the general colored population. Creole culture lost its special identity, the process extending to the language and to the music. The well-educated highly intelligent Creoles, traditionally schooled in the work ethic, began to abandon music in favor of more profitable endeavors. As Creoles left the music field they were replaced to some extent by colored bands based uptown, outside the Creole district. The most famous of them being the band led by Buddy Bolden. But a few brass bands continued the traditional parade music of New

271

Orleans until the mid-twentieth century, supported by a dwindling number of Creole and colored social clubs.

In 1911 it was still possible for Professor Manetta to assemble a band of Creole musicians to play in the Tuxedo Cabaret. By the early 1920s, however, Joe Oliver's "Creole" Band had only two members who were fluent in the Creole language. Even so, Oliver made sure the band operated by traditional and professional Creole dance music standards, carefully rehearsing their music and playing it the way it had been rehearsed. No amateurish improvising or faking was allowed in the Oliver band despite the theorizing of a multitude of jazz writers.

When music was permitted in the cabarets of Storyville, young white men, most of them without any knowledge of music, were able to listen to the sounds of Creole dance music for protracted periods. Their inept attempts to imitate those sounds resulted in the formation of routiner bands—the first derivation of New Orleans music. Calling themselves bands from dixieland, some of these faker bands later went to Chicago where, about 1915, their faked music was given the added appellation of jazz as an advertising feature, resulting in the name Dixieland Jazz.

A more earnest attempt to play the New Orleans style was made in the 1920s by Chicago youths who had a good understanding of music. These young white men heard New Orleans bands such as the Oliver band play in the dance halls of Chicago's South Side and were able to make a more serious evaluation of the qualities of the music. But they were unable to grasp the basic principles or to master the techniques of variation, instead often using the simple improvisation of faker bands. The result of their efforts became the second derivation of New Orleans music. Known as Chicago style, it had a short existence. Partly improvised and partly arranged, Chicago style quickly separated into the wholly improvised music of the jazz band or the wholly arranged music of the swing bands.

Throughout the 1920s swing music had been undergoing a process of development. The early years of the decade saw recordings made by A. J. Piron's New Orleans orchestra. This nine-piece Creole band, still led in the traditional manner by

Piron's violin, was patterned along the three division line of brass, reed and rhythm sections later followed by all swing bands.

Dancing became very popular in the 1920s and 1930s as the New Orleans style spread, resulting in the construction of large ballrooms with acoustic properties requiring larger bands. As the sections of the swing band expanded, sectional rehearsals became desirable to bring a smooth blending of the orchestration. The emphasis of discipline in the big bands, in addition to a lack of beat variation, sometimes resulted in a mechanical type of sound but the best of the swing bands—the bands that really did swing and played pleasant, orchestrated variations— were viewed with respect by the New Orleans musicians.

As the conditions of modern social life changed so the requirements for music altered. Functional music designed for various social activities declined in popularity after the second World War, therefore the demand for music based upon the principles of the New Orleans style also declined. It appears likely the two offshoots of the original music, dixieland jazz and swing, will retain a following for some indefinite time as indicated by recurrent revivalist periods. The simple imitative style of jazz bands consisting of little more than collective improvisation, a string of improvised solos and a mechanical-sounding beat has achieved acceptance on every continent, becoming a world style jazz. The more difficult big band swing music, requiring co-operation of skilled musicians and to a large extent dependent upon good orchestrations and careful rehearsals, may continue to serve a more limited market.

The New Orleans style, however, is not intended to be static or constrained to one or two modes of music, it can be suitable for all occasions. Properly understood and given the appropriate social conditions American music based on the principles of the New Orleans style could resume its long history of continuous development.

APPENDICES

APPENDIX I

Upon Marie Laveau's death the *Daily Picayune* carried an article eulogizing her. The date was June 16, 1881.

DEATH OF MARIE LAVEAU

A WOMAN WITH A WONDERFUL HISTORY, ALMOST A CENTURY OLD, CARRIED TO THE TOMB YESTERDAY EVENING

Those who have passed the quaint old house on St. Anne between Rampart and Burgundy streets with the high frail looking fence in front, over which a tree or two is visible, have till the last few years, noticed through the open gateway a decrepit old lady with snow white hair and a smile of peace and contentment lighting up her golden features. For a few years past she has been missed from her accustomed place. The feeble old lady lay upon her bed with her daughter and grandchildren around her ministering to her wants.

On Wednesday the invalid sank into the sleep which knows no waking. Those who she had befriended crowded into the little room where she was exposed, in order to obtain a last look at the features, smiling even in death, of her who had been so kind to them.

At 5 o'clock yesterday evening Marie Laveau was buried in her family tomb in St. Louis cemetery No. 1. Her remains were followed to the grave by a large concourse of people, the most prominent and most humble joining in paying their last respects to the dead. Father Mignot conducted the funeral services.

Marie Laveau was born sixty-eight years ago. Her father was a rich planter, who was prominent in all public affairs, and served in the legislature of this State. Her mother was Marguerite Henry, and her grandmother was Marguerite Semard. All were beautiful women of color. The gift of beauty was hereditary in the family and Marie inherited it in the fullest degree. When she was twenty-five years old she was led to the altar by Jacques Paris, a carpenter. Their marriage took place at the St. Louis Cathedral, Pierre Antione of beloved memory, conducting the service, and Mr. Jazurreau, the famous lawyer, acting as witness. A year afterward Mr. Paris disappeared and no one knows to this day what became of him. After waiting a year for his return she married Captain Christophe Glapion. The latter was also very prominent here and served with distinction in the battalion of men of San Domingo under D'Aquin, with Jackson in the war of 1815.

Fifteen children were the result of their marriage. Only one of these is now alive. Captain Glapion died greatly regretted, on the 26 June 1855. Five years afterwards Marie Laveau became ill, and has been sick ever since, her indisposition becoming more pronounced and painful within the last ten years.

Besides being very beautiful Marie was also very wise. She was skillful in the practice of medicine and was acquainted with the valuable healing qualities of indigenous herbs.

She was very successful as a nurse, wonderful stories being told of her exploits at the sick bed. In Yellow Fever and Cholera epidemics she was always called upon to nurse the sick and always responded promptly. Her skill and knowledge earned her the friendship and approbation of those sufficiently cultivated, but the ignorant attributed her success to unnatural means and held her in constant dread.

Notably in 1855 a committee of gentlemen appointed at a mass meting held at Globe Hall, waited on Marie and requested her on behalf of the people to minister to the fever stricken. She went out and fought the pestilence where it was thickest and many alive today owe their salvation to her devotion.

Not alone to the sick was Marie Laveau a blessing. To help a fellow creature in distress she considered a priceless privilege. She was born in the home where she died. Her mother lived and died there before her. The unassuming cottage has stood for a century and a half. It was built by the first French settlers of adobe and not a brick was employed in its construction. When it was erected it was considered the handsomest building in the neighborhood. Rampart street was not then in existence, being the skirt of a wilderness, and latterly a line of entrenchment. Notwithstanding the decay of her little mansion, Marie made the sight of it pleasant to the unfortunate. At any time of night or day anyone was welcome to food and lodging.

Those in trouble had but to come to her and she would make their cause her own often undergoing great sacrifices in order to assist them.

Besides being charitable, Marie was also very pious and took delight in strengthening the allegiance of souls to the church. She would sit with the condemned in their last moments and endeavor to turn their last thoughts to Jesus. Whenever a prisoner excited her pity Marie would labor incessantly to obtain his pardon, or at least a commutation of sentence, and she generally succeeded.

A few years ago, before she lost control of her memory she was rich in interesting reminiscences of the early history of this city. She spoke often of the young American Governor Claiborne, and told how the child-wife he brought with him from Tennessee died of the yellow fever shortly after his arrival, and with the dead babe upon her bosom was buried in a corner of the old American cemetery. She spoke sometimes of the strange little man with the wonderful bright eyes, Aaron Burr, who was so polite and so dangerous. She loved to talk of Lafayette, who visited New Orleans over half a century ago. The great Frenchman came to see her at her house and kissed her on the forehead at parting.

She remembered the old French general Humbert, and was one of the few colored people who escorted to the tomb, long since dismantled, in the Catholic cemetery, the withered and grizzled remains of the hero of Castelbar. Probably she knew Father Antoine better than any living in those days—for he the priest and she the nurse met at the dying bedside of hundreds of people—she to close the faded eyes in death and he to waft the soul over the river to the realms of eternal joy.

All in all Marie Laveau was a most wonderful woman. Doing good for the sake of doing good alone, she obtained no reward, oftimes meeting with prejudice and loathing, she was nevertheless contented and did not flag in her work. She always had the cause of the people at heart, and she was with them in all things. During the late rebellion she proved her loyalty to the South at every opportunity and freely dispensed help to those who suffered in defense of the "lost cause". Her last days were spent surrounded by sacred pictures and other evidences of religion, and she died with a firm trust in heaven. While God's sunshine plays around the little tomb where her remains are buried by the side of her second husband, and her sons and daughters, Marie Laveau's name will not be forgotten in New Orleans.

*　　*　　*

A few years after the death of Marie Laveau, George W. Cable began his imaginative writings concerning voodoo, Creole slaves(!) and Congo Square dances. One of several pusillanimous writers, under the protection of the racist regime and the Jim Crow laws, to disparage the oppressed people in general and Marie Laveau in particular. It was this type of fiction, reflecting the superstitions of many unconversant southern white people but posing as fact, that was to lay the basis for the African origin of jazz theory.

A reporter interviewed Marie's daughter, Madame Legendre, to inquire of her reaction to Cable's uncomplimentary remarks about her mother. Perhaps the reporter was the same writer that had eulogized Marie; almost certainly a Creole and possibly Paul Trevigne, who had a long career as a journalist in New Orleans.

The result was the following article printed in the *Daily Picayune* of April 11, 1886:

FLAGITIOUS FICTION

CABLE'S ROMANCE ABOUT MARIE LAVEAU AND THE VOUDOUS. HIS THRUSTS AT THE MEMORY OF ONE WHO DID WHAT GOOD SHE WAS ABLE TO DO.

A reporter made his debut as a reader yesterday before a small and select audience. The reading was from Cable and the listeners were the descendants of Marie Laveau, known as the Voudou Queen.

It was a striking group. The room was one looking out into the front yard of the quaint little old adobe dwelling down town on St. Ann Street. A rickety fence shuts out most of the view of the street, and the only glimpse of nature through the door are some struggling honeysuckle vines, tenderly nursed for their fragrance and also as a Creole remedy for sore throats. The room was the same in which Marie Laveau sat the long days through before her death. For many months ere she sank into her last sleep she sat in a rocking chair in the middle of the room, her eye resting on the holy images about her, the wrinkles on her bright yellow forehead deepening in thought, and snowy and abundant white hair covering a face which once glowed with the witchery of loveliness.

Those who read the face aright easily formed a true estimate of her life and character. Gifted with beauty and intelligence she ruled her own race, and made captives of many of the other. So large a number voluntarily came and confided in her that she became mistress of the secrets of many families—for the most influential families will have secrets, the discovery of which they own dread. This knowledge and her own shrewdness were the mystery of her power, just as they are of the power of others who lay claim to supernatural influence. As was to be expected in such a woman she was discreet. Her secrets died with her. What she knew was the unwritten history of New Orleans—more interesting and far more startling than any which has been told.

Marie Laveau was in some respects entitled to be called a queen. In her youth there were few more beautiful, and even in her old age her house was a castle. Low and narrow as it looks, its rambling sides hold many rooms and its walls have always harbored many of the needy and forsaken. The old man who Cable saw and describes as Marie's son was only an old retainer. The small, dark rooms have been the welcome refuge of scores of men and women, the history of whose lives would be romances stranger than any fathered in the imagination of the creator of "Madame Delphine". Even now there goes wearily to his rest, sad-eyed and broken-hearted, one who once held his head high among the merry leaders of life in the Crescent City.

Although it was an April day, there was a fire in Marie Laveau's old room. Around it sat M'me Legendre and three of her daughters, one of them with a chubby child across her lap. There are still three generations in the place.

Every one of the group was comely. M'me Legendre, although her heavy mass of hair is turning as white as that of her mother, still shows the sign of the beauty which she inherited. Tall, majestic, graceful, the eye still flashing fire, and with firm step notwithstanding months of illness, she rules her household, even if she has not the tact of Marie Laveau to extend her realm and number her subjects by the hundreds. This is what the reporter read to the group, in the little room of the old house, beside the fire that failed to brighten the walls but cast a glow upon the faces. It is from "Creole Slave Songs" in the April *Century*, by George W. Cable:

"The worship of Voudou is paid to a snake kept in a box. The worshippers are not merely a sect, but in some rude, savage way also an order. A man and woman, chosen from their own number to be the oracles of the serpent deity are called the king and queen. The queen is the more important of the two, and even in the present dilapidated state of the worship in Louisiana, where the king's office has almost or quite disappeared, the queen is still a person of great note. She reigns as long as she continues to live. She comes to power not by inheritance, but by election or its barbarous equivalent. Chosen for such qualities as would give her a natural supremacy, personal attraction among the rest, and ruling over superstitious fears and desires of every fierce and ignoble sort, she wields no trivial influence. I once saw, in her extreme old age, the famed Marie Laveau. Her dwelling was in a quadroon quarter of New Orleans, but a step or two from Congo Square, a small adobe cabin just off the sidewalk, scarcely higher than its close board fence, whose batten gate yielded to the touch and revealed the crazy doors and windows spread wide to the warm, and one or two tawny faces within, whose expression was divided between a pretense of contemptuous inattention and a frowning resent-

ment of the intrusion. In the center of a small room whose
ancient cypress floor was worn with scrubbing, crumbs of soft
brick—A Creole affectation of superior cleanliness—sat quak-
ing with feebleness in an ill-looking old rocking chair, her body
bowed, and her wild gray witch's tresses hanging about her
shriveled, yellow neck, the queen of the Voudous. Three generations of her children were with her in the faint beckon of her
helpless, waggling wrist and fingers. They said she was over a
hundred years old and there was nothing to cast doubt upon the
statement. She had shrunken away from her skin, it was like a
turtle's. Yet withal one could hardly help but see that the face,
now so withered, had once been handsome and commanding.
There was still a faint shadow of departed beauty on the forehead, the spark of an old fire in the sunken glistening eyes, and
a vestige of imperiousness in the fine slightly aquiline nose and
even about her silent, woebegone mouth. Her grandson stood by,
an uninteresting quadroon between forty and fifty years old
looking strong, empty minded and trivial enough; but his
mother, her daughter, was also present, a woman of some seventy years, and a most striking and majestic figure. In features,
stature and bearing she was regal. One had but to look on her,
impute her brilliance—too untamable and severe to be called
charms or graces—to her mother, and remember what New
Orleans was long years ago, to understand how the name of
Marie Laveau should have driven itself inextricably into the
traditions of the town and the times. Had this visit been post-
poned a few months it would have been too late. Marie Laveau is
dead; Malvina Latour is queen."

None of the four women waited until the reading was over.
Several times the reporter was interrupted by angry laughs of
derision and angry cries of "It's a lie. It's a lie." When the reading was over they were quite beside themselves with rage.
Madame Legendre was walking up and down the room with
quick, sharp steps, making vain attempts to express herself in
English, and then relapsing into scorching French. No attempt
is made to repeat her exact words.

"Snake in a box, indeed," cried M'me Legendre angrily,

"What for they say that about her when she is dead? She was too good. A great many people would not now hold up their heads so high if she had not been good. What did she know about a snake in a box? She worshipped God and went to church to say her prayers. I did that too until I was too sick, and now I pray at home," and she pointed to a wafer dimly burning. "It is all a lie from beginning to end. Nobody ever see her dance like that paper say. People have come here to see her and they never see anything wrong. I never could dance."

With teeth closed and lips quavering she walked across the narrow room, then appealing to the reporter:

"Can we not stop this? The courts must protect us. People come here and see nothing. They see nothing but ladies, and then they go off and they tell lies. My mother never did them any harm, and then they go off and write bad things about her. What they know? There are some men in this town who knew my mother and who have power. I will go and see them, and they will not then drag her name around and lie about her any more."

"But you cannot stop them from talking far away from home", suggested the reporter.

"Yes but I can tell them that they lie."

She was silent a moment, and the reporter told her about the engraving of Marie Laveau and herself, which accompanied the article.

"Her picture! My picture!" and she laughed bitterly. "That is a lie too. She never had her picture taken. They came often and asked her, but she never would. I am glad of it now, for they would have dragged that around also and put it in their lies. After her death an artist came to me and asked me to let him draw her. I told him that she was dead and he wanted me to let him copy some photograph. When I told him she never had any taken nor ever been sketched, he said what a pity."

She was quiet again for awhile and then commenced anew, but calmer than before.

"I know what we will do," she said to her daughters. "Hereafter we will let no one in. They had the excuse that the house was so old, and they wanted to see it. When they were polite we let them in. When we get money it will be an old house no more.

We will tear it down and build a new one. Then there will be nothing for them to see. Last year when there were so many people here many of them came down here to see the old house where Marie Laveau lived. One day a young man came down with a party of young ladies. He was very impertinent. He kept his hat on, and said he was coming in to look at the home. I told him to go to school and learn some manners first, and then shut the gate in his face. Two old gentlemen came, and they were so old and nice that I let them in. They were from the North, but had lived here when they were young and knew my mother very well. I let an artist in once and he drew the house and all the people in the yard. There are always plenty of people in the yard. They are glad enough to come here when they have nowhere to go and no place to sleep."

M'me Legendre had talked her anger away. She was weak from her exertions, and her illness made itself felt more than before. She talked in friendly tone, and even expressed a desire to see the last picture intended for her.

What M'me Legendre said about the few who were admitted recalled the efforts of various reporters to see Marie Laveau when she was alive. One had but to come and say that he wanted to "see the Voudou Queen" to open up all the batteries of wrath in the household. There was an active, little, talkative male relative who visited at the Laveau house, who assisted the women in compelling an enterprising journalist to leave almost by force. It is said that Cable himself was very unsuccessful in his mission, and that the only glimpse he ever obtained of Marie Laveau was very brief.

One fact about Marie Laveau has not been mentioned. She was deeply religious. Her house was filled with the pictures of saints and infant Saviours. A pretty altar was close beside her bed. When she had strength she was one of the most constant attendants at the Cathedral, and a model Catholic. Although she had taken none of the vows of a religious order, her heart prompted her to visit the Parish Prison whenever its walls held any unfortunate condemned to death. She labored earnest for the salvation of the souls of poor sinners such as those, built altars beside which she could pray with them, and went to them

285

often during the last days of their miserable life. Many remember her as a central figure at the triple execution which took place about fifteen years ago. Her strength was leaving her then, and she soon retired to the little room which she scarcely left until her death.

APPENDIX II

New Orleans Creole organizations represented at the funeral of Captain Andre Caillioux on July 11, 1863, included the following societies:

Francs Amis, Economie et Mutuelle Aide, Perseverance, Artisans, United Sisterhood, United Brotherhood, Union Sons Relief, Children of Mary, Children of Moses, Children of Jesus, La fleur de Marais, Ladies of Bon Secour, Arts and Mechanics, Friends of the Order, Star of the Cross, Good Shepard Conclave numbers One and Two, Angel Gabriel, God Protect Us, Well Beloved Sisters, Immaculate Conception, Sacred Union.

Also societies named after the following Saints:

Michael Archangel, Peter, Ann, Eulalie, Rose of Lima, Alphonsus, Magdalen, Louis Roi, Benoit, Theresa, Louis de Gonsaque, Joachim, Veronica.

INDEX

Gulber, G., 181

Handy, W.C., 4
Hardy, Emmett, 234
Henderson, Fletcher, 256
Hope's Hall, 101, 105, 178
Howard, Avery "Kid", 201
Howard, Joe, 226
Howard, Paul, 194, 201
Humphrey, J.B., 179, 184
Humphrey, Willie, Sr., 217
Hundred and One Ranch, The, 217, 218, 222
Hundred and Two Ranch, The, 218, 225, 227

Ida, 31
Imperial Orchestra, 250
Isiah, Ike "Peg Leg", 30

Jaeger, Charles, 151
James, Louis, 226
Jazzmen, 11, 12, 13, 22, 23
Jeunes Amis Hall, 101, 158
Johnson, Bill, 194, 253
Johnson, Buddy, 200
Johnson, Emma, 214, 215
Johnson, Jimmy, 33, 35
Jones, Chester, 200

Kelly, Thomas, 146, 148, 149, 151, 154
Keppard, Fred, 193, 194, 195, 217, 225
Keppard, Louis, 217
Kilshaw, George, 215, 217
Knights of Athens Society, 167, 168

Labatt, Alcide, 80
L'Abeille, 83
Lafon, Thomy, 80
Laine, Alfred, 233
Laine, Jack, 232, 233
Lala Cabaret, 227
Lambert, Billy, 235

Lambert, Lucien, 84, 85
Lamotte, Louisa, R., 83
Lanusse, Armand, 72, 74
Larocca, Nick, 3, 235, 237
Laussett, Pierre, 62
Laveau, Marie, 16, Appendix I
Leclerc, F., 181
Leesard, Joe, 200
Lenares, Ezab "Zeb", 226
Les Cenelles, 71, 72, 73, 74
Lewis, Danny, 36
Lewis, Frank, 28, 31, 32, 33, 36
Lincoln Gardens, 253
Loeper's Park, 163, 167, 168, 178
Longshoremen's Association, 180
Lopez, Ray, 235
Louisiana Five, The, 25
Love and Charity Hall, 35
Loyacano, Arnold, 235
L'Union, 136, 137
Lusitania Hall, 116
Lyceum Hall, 149
Lyre Musical Society, 181, 182

Macarty, Eugene, 86, 88, 89, 143, 144, 152
Macneil, Wendell, 250
Magnolia Gardens, 167
Manetta, Manuel, 27, 29, 30, 31, 33, 35, 36, 61, 184, 195, 214, 215, 217, 218, 219, 222, 224, 226, 234, 235
Mansion, L, 74
Mares, Paul, 236
Martin, Louis, professor, 154, 155, 179
Mary, Aristide, 80, 153
Mazurka, 6, 31, 62, 196
McCullum, George, Sr., 147
Mechanics Institute, 146, 148, 149
Mencken, H.L., 10, 53
Metoyer, Arnold, 219, 225
Mezzrow, Mezz, 238, 242, 252
Moret, Adolph, J. professor, 179, 184